# Building a Fireproof Church

## A Fresh Look at 1 Corinthians

James J. Burke

Fireproof Commentaries

Volume 1

**FIREPROOF**
COMMENTARIES

ISBN-13: 979-8-9941637-0-2

Cover design by: ChatGPT

Printed in the United States of America

fireproofcommentaries.org

*This work is dedicated to my first and greatest teacher, my pastoral mentor, and my favorite preacher — my Dad.*

# Table of Contents

# 1

## A Church in the Furnace of Corinth

### A Church in a Pagan City

The church at Corinth was born in a city of unparalleled wealth, brazen immorality, and entrenched idolatry, yet it became a shining beacon of God's grace. As we begin our study of 1 and 2 Corinthians, we explore how the Apostle Paul addressed the challenges of this vibrant yet deeply troubled congregation. His goal was not just to fix a few problems, but to build a fireproof church—a body of believers rooted in the gospel, united in purpose, and resilient against division. The Corinthian church faced issues that resonate deeply with churches today: divisions over personalities, moral compromise in the face of cultural pressure, and pride in human wisdom. Paul's letters offer timeless wisdom for overcoming these challenges, calling us to a radical unity found only in Christ.

This chapter introduces the context of Corinth, a city and a culture whose characteristics are essential to understanding Paul's message. We will trace Paul's journey to the city and his establishment of the church. We will then delve into the opening verses of 1 Corinthians 1, where Paul immediately confronts their disunity by calling them back to the very first principle of their faith: their shared identity in Christ as a community of saints. Through Paul's words, we will discover the ultimate foundation of a fireproof church: a shared calling to be holy, set apart, and united in the fellowship of Jesus Christ.

## The City of Corinth: A Challenging Mission Field

To grasp the challenges the Corinthian church faced, we must first understand the city of Corinth itself. It was no sleepy fishing village. Rebuilt by Julius Caesar in 44 BC, the city was a thriving Roman colony and a major trade hub at the crossroads of the Greek peninsula. Its unique geographical position, situated on a narrow isthmus with ports on both the Aegean and Ionian seas, funneled commerce across the Mediterranean, making it one of the wealthiest and most cosmopolitan cities in the Roman Empire. Its prosperity was fueled by a ruthless culture of competition and an infamous reputation for vice. The phrase "to act like a Corinthian" (*korinthiazesthai*) was a Greek byword for debauchery, a direct reference to the city's notorious temple of Aphrodite, which housed over a thousand sacred prostitutes.

Beyond the temples and taverns, Corinth was a city of fierce social stratification. A small, elite population of Roman citizens enjoyed significant legal and social privileges, while a vast underclass of slaves, laborers, and transient merchants jostled for position and survival. This created a culture where personal status, public reputation, and intellectual prowess were paramount. People in Corinth didn't just compete for money or power; they competed for recognition, to be seen, to be heard, and to be praised. This culture of one-upmanship was vividly displayed in the Isthmian Games, which were held in Corinth every two years, second only to the Olympics in prestige. These games brought fame-seeking athletes, ambitious orators, and spectators from across the Roman world, reinforcing a spirit of fierce, individualistic competition.

In this environment, Paul's message of a crucified, humble Savior was deeply countercultural. The gospel calls for self-denial and unity, the opposite of a city built on self-promotion and individual achievement. God chose this unlikely, prideful place to establish a community that would reflect His light in the darkness, a stark and powerful testament to the gospel's ability to transform even the most challenging of hearts and cultures.

# Corinth as a Roman Colony: A Deeper Look

To understand the social and economic fabric of Corinth, we must explore its status as a Roman colony. In 44 BC, Julius Caesar refounded the city, which had been destroyed by the Romans a century earlier. The city was repopulated with a large number of Roman freedmen and veterans who were granted land and citizenship. This strategic move was not just a rebuilding effort; it was a deliberate act of cultural and political colonization. This Roman foundation had profound implications for the social and economic life of the city.

Socially, the city was a microcosm of Roman society, with a clear hierarchy. The top tier consisted of Roman citizens, who held the most power and wealth. They had the right to vote in local elections, own property, and be tried under Roman law. Below them were the Greek inhabitants and a large population of slaves and freedmen. This social divide was a constant source of tension. The Roman citizens, proud of their status, would have looked down on the Greek culture that surrounded them, even as they benefited from its economic prosperity. The local church, a mix of both Roman citizens and Greek freedmen and slaves, was a radical social experiment. A Roman citizen and a Greek slave were now brothers and sisters in Christ, an unheard-of concept in the Roman world.

Economically, Corinth's colonial status made it a hub for Roman trade and commerce. Roman veterans brought with them agricultural knowledge and an appreciation for Roman luxuries. The city was rebuilt with Roman infrastructure, including a Roman-style forum, temples, and theaters. The Isthmus, the narrow strip of land connecting the Peloponnese to mainland Greece, was a crucial trade route. Instead of sailing the dangerous journey around the peninsula, many ships would unload their goods at one port, have them carried across the isthmus, and reloaded onto another ship on the other side. This created an incredibly wealthy and bustling economy, but it also fostered a culture of cutthroat competition. People in Corinth were driven by money and status, and their spiritual lives were often an extension of this worldly ambition. The factions in the church—I am of Paul, I am of Apollos—were a direct reflection of this culture, where people sought to align themselves with a powerful leader to gain status and influence. Paul's message, which called for a rejection of this worldly pride and a focus on a crucified Savior, was a radical call to a different kind of kingdom.

# Paul's Journey: God's Provision in Adversity

Paul's path to Corinth, detailed in Acts 16–18, was not a triumphant march but a series of trials that tested his faith and prepared him for the work ahead. His journey began in Troas, where a vision of a Macedonian man led him to Philippi. There, he founded a church with Lydia, a businesswoman who sold purple, but faced severe persecution, being beaten and imprisoned. Enduring hardship in Thessalonica and Berea, Paul finally arrived in Athens. He tried a different strategy, engaging the city's intellectual elite at the Areopagus, using their philosophical framework to present the gospel. Yet, his message about the resurrection of the dead was largely mocked, yielding few converts. Paul left Athens feeling discouraged, alone, and without a clear plan.

It was in this state of weariness that he arrived in Corinth. He didn't arrive as a conquering hero but as a humbled servant, and God, in His perfect providence, had a plan for his weakness. He provided Paul with Aquila and Priscilla, Jewish Christians who had been expelled from Rome by Emperor Claudius's decree. As tentmakers, they shared Paul's trade, offering him work, lodging, and much-needed fellowship. This seemingly small provision was a profound act of grace. It grounded Paul's ministry, allowing him to preach every Sabbath, earning a living so he would not be a financial burden to the fledgling church. God used Paul's weakness and loneliness as an opportunity to demonstrate His faithfulness, showing that His work is built not on human strength or intellectual prowess, but on His divine provision. This was the foundation of the Corinthian church, one built by a man at his wit's end, sustained by God's grace.

## Paul's Relationship with Corinth: A Journey of Grace and Correction

Paul's 18-month ministry in Corinth laid the groundwork for a vibrant yet flawed church, with converts like Crispus, the ruler of the synagogue, and Gaius, a Roman nobleman. His relationship with the Corinthians extended far beyond his initial stay, marked by multiple letters and visits to address division, immorality, and false teaching. This complex engagement—founding, correcting, confronting, and reconciling—shows Paul's pastoral heart and models the resilience of a fireproof church.

**The First Letter (The "Lost Letter"):** Before 1 Corinthians, Paul wrote an earlier letter, referenced in 1 Corinthians 5:9: "I wrote unto you in an epistle not to company with fornicators" (KJV). This "lost letter" reveals Paul's early concern for their holiness, urging them to separate from blatant sin. Its absence from the canon suggests it was a specific, timely correction, setting the stage for the more comprehensive letter that would follow.

**The Second Letter (1 Corinthians):** Written from Ephesus around 55 AD, 1 Corinthians responds to reports from Chloe's household about divisions and addresses questions from the church. Paul tackles a wide range of issues, from factionalism and sexual immorality to lawsuits and the proper use of spiritual gifts, all while calling for unity and maturity. This letter establishes the vision of a fireproof church built on Christ crucified.

**The Painful Visit:** After 1 Corinthians, Paul made an unplanned, "painful" visit to Corinth. He came in "heaviness," likely to confront a specific offender or persistent divisions. This visit was met with resistance, possibly from members who questioned his apostolic authority. The rejection deepened his sorrow, prompting a further letter.

**The Severe Letter:** Following the painful visit, Paul wrote a "severe letter," mentioned in 2 Corinthians 7:8. Written with anguish and tears, this letter confronted ongoing sin or opposition, possibly from false teachers undermining Paul's apostleship. Its strong message led to repentance among the majority, paving the way for reconciliation.

**2 Corinthians:** Written around 56–57 AD, 2 Corinthians reflects Paul's relief at Corinth's repentance. In this letter, he defends his apostolic ministry against false apostles, encourages generosity for the Jerusalem collection, and addresses suffering and unity. This letter completes Paul's journey with Corinth, from correction to restoration, modeling a fireproof church's endurance.

Paul's persistent engagement, despite Corinth's flaws, mirrors God's grace. His love for the church, through trials and rejection, reflects Christ's heart for His body.

# The Corinthian Church: A Call to Unity

The Corinthian church, though troubled, was a powerful testament to God's power. Paul's ministry there saw the conversion of Crispus, the synagogue leader, and others, despite Jewish opposition. Remarkably, Sosthenes, the new synagogue leader who opposed Paul, was later converted, co-authoring 1 Corinthians. This transformation—from persecutor to partner—illustrates God's power to redeem even our greatest opponents.

Paul's first letter to Corinth begins by affirming his calling as an apostle, chosen by Christ on the Damascus road. He addresses the church as "sanctified in Christ Jesus, called to be saints" (1

Corinthians 1:2, KJV), a powerful reminder of their corporate identity. The Greek word *ekklēsia* (church) means a "called-out assembly," a community set apart for Christ, not a building or a social club. The term "saints," always plural in Scripture, reflects the collective holiness of believers, sanctified by Christ's righteousness. This is a crucial point for a church plagued by division: their primary identity wasn't as a follower of Paul or Apollos, but as a member of God's holy, called-out people.

Paul's plea for unity is urgent: "that ye all speak the same thing, and that there be no divisions among you; but that ye be perfectly joined together in the same mind and in the same judgment." (1 Corinthians 1:10, KJV). Unity, not uniformity, is the goal, achieved by sharing the mind of Christ. He reminds them that the source of their gifts is Christ, not themselves, and that their calling transcends their individual differences. This unity challenges churches today, which are often split by loyalty to charismatic leaders or political camps, reminding us that Christ alone is our head.

## The Call to Be Saints: A Shared Identity in Christ

The Corinthians were divided over personalities, sin, status, and doctrine. Paul's solution is to root their identity in their calling as saints. This calling is not earned but received through faith in Christ.

William Tyndale understood this truth when he labored to translate the Scriptures into English. His most controversial choice was rendering *ekklēsia* not as "church" but as "congregation." To the authorities, "church" safeguarded the institution—bishops, priests, and hierarchy. "Congregation," however, emphasized the gathered people of God, ordinary believers called out by Christ. This single word undermined centuries of ecclesiastical control, and for it Tyndale was condemned as a heretic and ultimately martyred.

Tyndale's witness reminds us that saints are not solitary superstars but a community reflecting Christ's holiness together. This calling is not contingent on acceptance but on faithfulness. When we share the gospel and face rejection, we are not rejected—God is. This frees us to serve boldly, trusting God's grace. It is this shared calling that binds a fireproof church together, making it resilient against the forces of division from within and without.

## Application: Building a Fireproof Church

A fireproof church is united in its calling to Christ. Here are four ways to apply this truth:

- **Embrace Your Calling**: Recognize that God has called you to His church, not to try Jesus out but to serve Him faithfully. Your presence in the body is purposeful, equipped by God's gifts for His glory (Ephesians 4:1).

- **Reject Division**: Divisions over preachers, status, or preferences weaken the church. As Paul urges, "be perfectly joined together" in the mind of Christ, found in His Word (1 Corinthians 1:10, KJV).

- **Serve Together**: As saints, we are called to fellowship, not isolation. Support one another, as Aquila and Priscilla supported Paul, and trust God to use you where He places you.

- **Persevere in Faith**: Like Paul through trials, trust God's provision amid rejection or hardship. Share the gospel boldly, knowing He sustains you, and remember that our calling is secure in Him, regardless of the outcome.

## Conclusion: A Unified Body

A fireproof church is built on the calling to be saints, united in Christ. Corinth's pagan culture could not extinguish the gospel's light, nor can ours. Let us link arms, love one another, and serve faithfully, knowing that God has called us to His body. As we study 1 and 2 Corinthians, may we learn from Paul's perseverance and build a church that glorifies Christ alone.

## Prayer

*Father, we thank You for calling us to be Your saints. Teach us to rest in our calling, reject division, and serve together. Build us into a fireproof church that reflects Your glory. In Jesus' name,*

*Amen.*

# 2

# Called to the Cross: Overcoming Division

## The Danger of Division

The Corinthian church, though richly gifted, was fracturing under the weight of division. We have discussed the disagreements over personality, preference, social position, and moral failure that were creating factions that threatened the church's witness. In 1 Corinthians 1, Paul confronts this disunity, calling the church to anchor its identity in the cross of Christ. This chapter explores how the cross destroys division and builds a fireproof church, one united not by human wisdom or personalities but by the power of God.

## The Corinthian Crisis

Paul's letter to the Corinthians, written around 55 AD from Ephesus, was prompted by a report from Chloe's household about "contentions" in the church (1 Corinthians 1:11, KJV). The Corinthians boasted in their gifts—eloquence, knowledge, and spiritual experiences—but their pride fueled rivalries. Some claimed Paul, the church's founder; others preferred Apollos, the eloquent Alexandrian; some followed Cephas (Peter), the original apostle; and others, claiming superior spirituality, said, "I am of Christ" (1 Corinthians 1:12).

These divisions mirrored the city's competitive culture, where status and rhetoric reigned. The Corinthians were conditioned to choose sides, to align with a particular school of philosophy or a favored orator. For them, a church leader was like a celebrity philosopher, and following him was a sign of intellectual or spiritual superiority. This obsession with human wisdom and performance directly opposed the message of the cross. A church that prides itself on the eloquence of its pastor or the size of its brand is a church that has forgotten its foundation. It is a church built on the fleeting value of human charisma, not the enduring power of the gospel.

Paul's response is a passionate plea for unity, rooted in the gospel.

> *"Paul, called to be an apostle of Jesus Christ through the will of God, and Sosthenes our brother, unto the church of God which is at Corinth, to them that are sanctified in Christ Jesus, called to be saints… Now I beseech you, brethren, by the name of our Lord Jesus*

*Christ, that ye all speak the same thing, and that there be no divisions among you; but that ye be perfectly joined together in the same mind and in the same judgment. For it hath been declared unto me of you, my brethren, by them which are of the house of Chloe, that there are contentions among you. Now this I say, that every one of you saith, I am of Paul; and I of Apollos; and I of Cephas; and I of Christ. Is Christ divided? Was Paul crucified for you? or were ye baptized in the name of Paul? I thank God that I baptized none of you, but Crispus and Gaius; lest any should say that I had baptized in mine own name. And I baptized also the household of Stephanas: besides, I know not whether I baptized any other. For Christ sent me not to baptize, but to preach the gospel: not with wisdom of words, lest the cross of Christ should be made of none effect. For the preaching of the cross is to them that perish foolishness, but unto us which are saved it is the power of God... But of him are ye in Christ Jesus, who of God is made unto us wisdom, and righteousness, and sanctification, and redemption: that, according as it is written, He that glorieth, let him glory in the Lord." (1 Corinthians 1:1–31, KJV)*

# Apollos and the Culture of Rhetoric: When Style Trumps Substance

Central to Corinth's factions was Apollos, a figure whose eloquence sparked admiration but unwittingly fueled disunity. Acts 18:24–28 describes him as "an eloquent man, and mighty in the scriptures," hailing from Alexandria, a renowned center of learning. Alexandria was famous for its great library and a tradition of Jewish scholarship that blended Greek philosophy and biblical study, a school of thought exemplified by the Jewish philosopher Philo. Apollos's training equipped him to teach with clarity and power.

To the Corinthians, Apollos was not just a preacher; he was a *rhetor*, an orator. In the Greco-Roman world, the art of rhetoric was a high-status profession. Orators, known as *sophists*, were celebrities who commanded large audiences and fees. They were masters of style, wit, and logical argument, using their verbal gymnastics to win debates and influence public opinion. The Corinthians, steeped in this culture, naturally valued Paul and Apollos based on their rhetorical skill. Apollos, with his polished, philosophical style, was seen as superior to Paul, whose preaching was "not with excellency of speech or of wisdom" (1 Corinthians 2:1, KJV).

This mirrors a modern phenomenon where believers rally behind celebrity pastors with large online followings or dynamic sermon styles, mistaking charisma for spiritual authority. Apollos was not the problem—his ministry was godly—but the Corinthians' pride turned a gift into a stumbling block. As Gordon Fee notes, "Apollos' eloquence, a divine gift, became a source of division when human wisdom trumped gospel unity." This obsession with a speaker's style over the message's substance is a timeless threat to a fireproof church.

## The Cross: The Cure for Division

Paul's plea for unity is urgent: "that ye all speak the same thing, and that there be no divisions among you." The Greek word for divisions, *schismata*, suggests tears in a garment, repairable only by the cross. Paul asks, "Is Christ divided? Was Paul crucified for you?" (1 Corinthians 1:13, KJV). No human leader died for the church; only Christ.

Baptism, an outward symbol of inward faith, identifies us with Christ, not a preacher. Paul's statement, "I thank God that I baptized none of you," underscores that his mission was to preach the gospel, not to build a following.

The cross, not human eloquence, is the power of God. To the perishing, the cross is foolishness; to the saved, it is God's power. Quoting Isaiah 29:14, Paul declares that God confounds human wisdom: "I will destroy the wisdom of the wise, and will bring to nothing the understanding of the prudent" (1

Corinthians 1:19, KJV). Jews sought signs, Greeks wisdom, but the cross—a stumbling block to Jews and folly to Greeks—is God's wisdom and power to those called. God chooses the foolish and weak to shame the wise and mighty, ensuring no one glories in themselves.

## The Cross: A Stumbling Block to the Jew

From the Jewish perspective, the cross was the ultimate sign of a curse, as written in Deuteronomy 21:23: "he that is hanged on a tree is accursed of God." For a devout Jew, the idea of a crucified Messiah was an absurd contradiction.

They expected a triumphant, conquering King who would lead an army to victory against Rome and restore Israel's glory. A suffering, dying, publicly shamed Messiah was a complete impossibility. It was a scandal that shattered their expectations and defied their understanding of a powerful God. The cross was a direct affront to their national and religious pride. It was a stumbling block over which many of them fell.

## A Sign of Contradiction: The Sign of Jonah

Paul's message of the cross as a "stumbling block" to the Jews is best understood in light of their demand for a sign. In Matthew 12:38, the scribes and Pharisees ask Jesus for a sign to prove His authority, and His response is profound and chilling: "An evil and adulterous generation seeketh after a sign; and there shall no sign be given to it, but the sign of the prophet Jonah: for as Jonas was three days and three nights in the whale's belly; so shall the Son of man be three days and three nights in the heart of the earth" (KJV).

The Jews were looking for a sign of power and triumph—a miracle that would demonstrate Jesus's authority over Rome and validate their nationalist aspirations. They wanted a sign that affirmed their own desires for a political Messiah. But Jesus offered them the sign of Jonah, a sign of death, burial, and resurrection. This was not the sign they wanted, because it was a sign they could not control. It was a sign of humility, a sign that required faith, and a sign that pointed to a Messiah who would die for their sins, not a king who would kill their enemies.

They rejected the sign of Jonah because it did not fit their preconceived notions of a triumphant Messiah. They were so blinded by their own desires that they could not see the very thing that would save them. This rejection culminated in their rejection of the risen Christ. They had every opportunity to believe—from the empty tomb to the witness of the disciples—but their hearts, hardened by their desire for a different kind of king, would not allow them to accept a resurrected Savior who had defeated sin and death, not Rome.

## The Cross: Folly to the Greeks

For the Greeks, who valued physical perfection, philosophical ideals, and self-mastery, the cross was an object of utter shame and intellectual absurdity. Crucifixion was the most despised form of execution, reserved for slaves, traitors, and the lowest criminals. It was a brutal, public, and demeaning punishment. A God-man who would willingly submit to such a humiliating and weak death was a joke. It was the antithesis of their *logos* (reason) and their quest for a philosophical life free from worldly attachments and passions. By choosing a crucified Savior, God took the symbols of shame and weakness and turned them into the ultimate expression of His power and glory.

This paradox remains today. A secular world, obsessed with power, self-reliance, and human progress, finds the cross a relic of a primitive, shameful past. But a fireproof church understands that what the world sees as a scandal is in fact the glorious display of God's love and power.

# A Deeper Look at Luke 16: The Refusal to Believe

The parable of the rich man and Lazarus provides a chilling illustration of this human refusal to believe. After the rich man dies and is in torment, he begs Abraham to send Lazarus back from the dead to warn his five brothers, so they will not suffer the same fate. Abraham's reply is a profound commentary on the human heart: "If they hear not Moses and the Prophets, neither will they be persuaded, though one rose from the dead" (Luke 16:31, KJV).

This verse is a direct answer to the Jewish demand for a sign. The rich man's brothers had Moses and the Prophets—the written Word of God—but they had rejected it. They had all the information they needed to believe, but they chose not to. And Abraham's point is that even a sign as dramatic and undeniable as a resurrection would not change their minds. They would find a way to explain it away, to deny it, or to dismiss it, because their problem was not a lack of information; their problem was a heart of unbelief.

This is a prophetic word for the Jewish rejection of Christ. They had seen signs—Jesus walking on water, healing the sick, and even raising people from the dead—and yet they demanded more. They had Moses and the Prophets, who testified to the coming Messiah, and yet they rejected Him. Their final, and most profound, rejection was of the risen Christ. The eyewitnesses were there. The empty tomb was there. But just as Abraham predicted, they would not be persuaded, because their heart's desire was a political savior, not a spiritual one. Their rejection of the sign of Jonah—the resurrection—was the final act of their unbelief, proving that their heart's desire was not truth, but power. The cross was a stumbling block for them because it defied their desire for a king who would conquer, not a king who would die.

## Isaiah 29:14: God's Mysterious Work

Paul's use of Isaiah 29:14 anchors the cross in God's redemptive plan. In this prophecy, God promises a "marvellous work" that would be incomprehensible to the wise. This "marvellous work" was not a human solution to human problems; it was a divine solution that defied all expectations. This is the very nature of the cross. What looks like defeat is victory; what appears weak is strength; what seems foolish is the very wisdom of God.

Today, churches chasing cultural relevance or social media metrics mirror Israel's trust in worldly wisdom. They may find temporary success, but a gospel diluted to fit a market will lack the power of God. The cross remains God's mysterious, unifying power, the only answer to a divided world.

# The Gospel's Power: Christ Our Wisdom

The cross is God's answer to division because it redefines wisdom, righteousness, sanctification, and redemption (1 Corinthians 1:30). Human wisdom seeks signs or eloquence, but God chose the cross. Consider the Corinthians' backgrounds: "Not many wise men after the flesh, not many mighty, not many noble" (1 Corinthians 1:26, KJV). God chose fishermen, tax collectors, and sinners like the Philippian jailer or Corinth's own Sosthenes—to shame the proud. This echoes Jesus' ministry, calling unlikely disciples. In the 21st Century, God still calls the ordinary—factory workers, teachers, or recovering addicts—to build His church, not influencers with large platforms.

The gospel ensures no one boasts in themselves: "He that glorieth, let him glory in the Lord" (1 Corinthians 1:31, KJV, citing Jeremiah 9:24). The cross levels the playing field, uniting diverse believers—rich, poor, Jew, Gentile—in Christ's righteousness. In a polarized world, where churches divide over politics or preacher popularity, the cross calls us to humility and unity.

## Conclusion: Christ, Our Identity

The cross destroys division by uniting us in Christ. Whether you follow Paul, Apollos, or another, your identity is in the One who died for you. Let Christ's image shine through you, and walk together as His body. A fireproof church is one where every member serves Christ, not self, creating a witness that endures.

## Application: Unity in the Cross

A fireproof church rejects division and embraces the cross. Here are four applications to build such a church:

- **Center on Christ**: Avoid exalting preachers or personalities, as Charles Swindoll notes: "The church is not a fan club for preachers but a body united in Christ." Reject loyalty to celebrity pastors or online influencers, focusing on the cross.

- **Live Your Calling**: God calls the unlikely—those not wise or noble by worldly standards. Serve faithfully where God places you, trusting His gifts, not your resume.

- **Pursue Harmony**: Unity is not uniformity but harmony, like a choir singing different notes in accord. Study God's Word to align with Christ's mind, fostering unity despite differences (Philippians 2:5).

- **Embrace the Cross's Foolishness**: The cross defies worldly logic, like chasing social media clout or cultural relevance. Trust its power to transform hearts, rejecting prideful divisions.

## Prayer

*Father, imprint Christ's image on us. May we reject division, embrace our calling, and walk in unity. Build us into a fireproof church that glorifies You. In Jesus' name,*

*Amen.*

# 3

## The Wisdom of the Cross

### A Message of Power in Weakness

When Paul arrived in Corinth, he was weary, broken, and alone, yet God used his weakness to plant a church that would shine in a pagan city. The Corinthian church, though gifted, was swayed by human wisdom, chasing eloquence and status over the gospel. In 1 Corinthians 1:17–2:10, Paul counters this with the wisdom of the cross—a message that seems foolish to the world but is God's power to save. This chapter explores how the cross, not human philosophy, builds a fireproof church, united and resilient against the allure of worldly wisdom. In the 21st century, as churches face pressures from social media spirituality and self-help trends, Paul's call to cling to the cross remains urgent, offering the only true hope for salvation and unity.

### Paul's Weakness in Corinth

Paul's journey to Corinth, detailed in Acts 16–18, was a series of humbling trials. In Philippi, he was publicly beaten and imprisoned. In Thessalonica, he was chased out by an angry mob. In Berea, he found a brief welcome, but opposition followed. In Athens, he found a city of philosophers and idols, and he attempted a different approach. He preached a reasoned sermon at the Areopagus, engaging their worldview by quoting Greek poets. While some listened and a few believed, the effort yielded no lasting church. By the time Paul entered Corinth, he was deeply discouraged, broke, and alone. He later admitted he came "in weakness and in fear and much trembling" (1 Corinthians 2:3, KJV). The Greek word *phobos* here indicates a profound sense of dread. After his failures in other cities, he was vulnerable, anxious, and alone, but he continued to press on.

Yet God did not abandon him. In Corinth, he met Aquila and Priscilla, Jewish Christian tentmakers expelled from Rome. Their shared trade provided work, fellowship, and stability, enabling Paul to preach every Sabbath. This was God's gracious provision, grounding Paul's ministry and ensuring his message was not about a polished performance, but a simple, life-changing truth. Over 18 months, God, in His power, brought converts like Crispus and Sosthenes to the fledgling community. Paul's weakness in Corinth was God's opportunity to display His power. His reliance on God, not on human strength or intellectual prowess, proved that faith should not stand in the wisdom of men, but in the power of God.

This was a critical lesson for the Corinthian church, which soon found its members swayed by the very human wisdom Paul had rejected.

## The Corinthian Challenge: A Church Divided

Corinth's church, born in a city of wealth and vice, mirrored its culture's obsession with rhetoric and prestige. Members boasted in their gifts—eloquence, knowledge, spiritual experiences—and aligned with favorite leaders: Paul, the founder; Apollos, the eloquent Alexandrian; Cephas (Peter), the apostle; or Christ, claiming superior spirituality. This echoed today's churches, where divisions form over celebrity pastors, viral sermon clips, or political alignments. Paul's answer was sharp: the gospel rests not on human wisdom but on the cross.

*"For Christ sent me not to baptize, but to preach the gospel: not with wisdom of words, lest the cross of Christ should be made of none effect. For the preaching of the cross is to them that perish foolishness, but unto us which are saved it is the power of God... But of him are ye in Christ Jesus, who of God is made unto us wisdom, and righteousness, and sanctification, and redemption: that, according as it is written, He that glorieth, let him glory in the Lord." (1 Corinthians 1:17–2:10, KJV)*

Paul's mission was clear: preach "Jesus Christ, and him crucified" (1 Corinthians 2:2, KJV), not with dazzling rhetoric, but with a simple, Spirit-empowered message. This message challenges two pillars: human wisdom's failure and the cross's divine wisdom.

## Pillar One: The Failure of Human Wisdom

Paul learned this in Athens. His sermon, while intellectually sound, was ultimately ineffective. He engaged their philosophy, but when he preached the resurrection, most scoffed. Human wisdom, even at its best, cannot lead to God. It raises profound questions but lacks the answers for sin and reconciliation. It can offer coping mechanisms, but it can never truly solve the human condition.

To understand why, we return to Eden. Adam's sin was not a stumble but a conscious rebellion. He deliberately disobeyed God, choosing to "be as gods, knowing good and evil" (Genesis 3:5, KJV). This was a willful rejection of God's rule. Humanity inherited this rebellious nature, a condition that no amount of philosophy, education, or self-help can fix. As Leon Morris observes, "Sin is not a problem to be solved by reason but a condition requiring divine redemption." Secular worldviews today—from self-optimization apps to social justice reforms—promise transformation but fail to address sin's root, leaving humanity with guilt and despair.

Jesus' parable of the rich man and Lazarus illustrates this further. The rich man, in torment, begged Abraham to send a resurrected Lazarus to warn his brothers. Abraham replied, "If they hear not Moses and the Prophets, neither will they be persuaded, though one rose from the dead" (Luke 16:31, KJV). The point is clear: sight is not faith.

Miracles and intellectual proofs cannot compel belief without the Spirit and the Word. Human wisdom demands proof, but faith comes through hearing the gospel. Today's obsession with TED Talks or viral spiritual gurus mirrors this, offering insights but no salvation.

## Pillar Two: The Power of God's Wisdom in the Cross

If human wisdom fails, God's wisdom triumphs through the cross. Paul's preaching in Corinth avoided "enticing words of man's wisdom" (1 Corinthians 2:4, KJV), relying instead on the Spirit's power. The cross seems foolish—a crucified Messiah was a scandal to Jews and folly to Greeks, who saw crucifixion as a slave's death. Yet, to those called, it is "the power of God, and the wisdom of God" (1 Corinthians 1:24, KJV).

The cross inverts human expectations. Jews sought a conquering Messiah, Greeks a philosophical ideal, but God chose a crucified Savior. What looks like defeat is victory; what seems weak is strength. As Anthony Thiselton writes, "The cross subverts human pride, revealing God's wisdom in apparent foolishness." In the 21st Century, churches chasing cultural relevance —through polished livestreams or self-help sermons —risk diluting this paradox, making the gospel palatable but powerless. Paul rejected eloquent wisdom to preserve the cross's power. In 1 Corinthians 1:17, the Greek word for "of none effect," κενόω (kenōō), is often used to describe "hollowing out", as Christ himself did by leaving His divine glory in Philippians 2:7, and this is exactly what happens when the gospel is stripped of its power; its glory is gone. Eloquence is not sinful, but it can obscure the message, making preaching a performance, like a watermelon rind—outwardly whole but hollow inside. A gospel without the cross is attractive but empty, like modern spiritualities promising peace without repentance.

The cross addresses sin's gravity. Imagine a courtroom: humanity, like Adam, stands guilty, sentenced to death. No excuse—ignorance, good works, or plea bargains—avails. Christ enters, not to argue innocence but to take our guilt. The Judge becomes the sacrifice, declaring us righteous through faith. This is God's wisdom: justice and mercy meet at the cross, uniting believers in Christ's redemption.

The cross's power shines in the Philippian jailer. Beaten and chained, Paul and Silas sang hymns. An earthquake freed them, but they stayed, sparing the jailer's life.

Trembling, he asked, "What must I do to be saved?" (Acts 16:30, KJV). Paul's reply—"Believe on the Lord Jesus Christ, and thou shalt be saved" (Acts 16:31, KJV)—led to his family's conversion and baptism. Not miracles or eloquence, but the cross, empowered by the Spirit, saved him. This echoes John 16:13, where the Spirit guides into truth, applying the gospel to hearts.

Paul's preaching relied on "demonstration of the Spirit and of power" (1 Corinthians 2:4, KJV). This demonstration was not necessarily a display of miracles, but the working of the Holy Spirit to bring the truth of the gospel home to the hearts of the hearers. As Paul states in Romans 1:16, the gospel is the δύναμις (*dynamis*), or "power," of God unto salvation —the same Greek root from which we get the English word "dynamo." It was not human wisdom or clever rhetoric but spiritual truth applied spiritually that wrought conversion. Without the Spirit, even resurrection appearances can produce doubt. With the Spirit, simple truths transform lives. The Spirit reveals "the deep things of God" (1 Corinthians 1:10,

KJV), making the cross's wisdom clear to those called. As N. T. Wright notes, "The Spirit bridges the gap between human blindness and divine truth."

## A Coherent Christian Worldview

Human worldviews—ancient philosophy or modern secularism—cannot explain evil, guilt, or death. They offer coping mechanisms or despair. The cross provides a coherent worldview: sin explains the world's brokenness; guilt reflects our rebellion; death is sin's wage; and hope comes through Christ's sacrifice and resurrection. This worldview humbles us: our wisdom is worthless. It saves us: Christ's righteousness becomes ours. It reshapes us: the Spirit renews our desires. It sends us: we proclaim Christ crucified, trusting God's power. In the 21st century, as churches face pressure to adopt self-help gospels or social media metrics, the cross remains the only foundation for a fireproof church, uniting believers in truth.

The cross defies human logic. If tasked with solving sin's debt—"the soul that sinneth, it shall die" (Ezekiel 18:20, KJV)—we might rely on good deeds or rituals. Yet, no effort erases past sin. I once met a woman who claimed only seven sins in 97 years. Even if true, seven sins require atonement, available only through the cross. Adam's rebellion was a choice, and God's heartbroken response allowed humanity's desire while

34

protecting us from eternal suffering. God's plan—the Creator dying for His creation—is so radical it seems foolish. Yet, as Romans 5:8 declares, "while we were yet sinners, Christ died for us." This love, incomprehensible to the world, is the wisdom that builds a fireproof church.

## Conclusion: Glory in the Cross

The wisdom of the cross unites and empowers the church. By rejecting human wisdom and embracing Christ's sacrifice, we build a fireproof church that endures. Let us glory in the Lord, trusting His wisdom to guide us.

## Application: Living the Wisdom of the Cross

A fireproof church embraces the cross's wisdom over human pride. Here are four ways to apply this truth:

- **Cling to the Cross**: Reject eloquent trends—self-help sermons or viral spirituality—that dilute the gospel. Center on Christ crucified, the power of God.

- **Trust the Spirit**: Rely on the Spirit's work through the Word, not human charisma or cultural relevance, to transform hearts.

- **Embrace Weakness**: Like Paul in weakness, trust God's strength in your limitations. Serve faithfully, knowing He uses the humble.

- **Proclaim the Gospel**: Share Christ crucified boldly, despite worldly scorn, trusting its power to save.

# Prayer

*Father, thank You for the wisdom of the cross. May we trust Your Spirit, reject worldly wisdom, and build a church that glories in You. In Jesus' name,*

*Amen.*

# 4

## The Foundation of a Fireproof Church

### The Heart of a Fireproof Church

In the previous chapters, we saw how the Corinthian church, though richly gifted, was being torn apart by divisions over human leaders. Paul, however, shifts their focus from the builders to the very foundation itself. In 1 Corinthians 3, he reveals a powerful truth about building a fireproof church: it must be built on one foundation, and one only—Jesus Christ. This chapter is a solemn call for us to examine our own lives and our churches. For when the fires of tribulation come, what we have built will be tested, and only that which is genuine will endure. By examining our hearts and our work, we ensure the church stands firm, united in Christ, as a beacon of His grace in a divided world.

# The Corinthian Crisis: Division and Spiritual Infancy

The Corinthian church was filled with contention. Members aligned themselves with favorite preachers —Paul, the church's founder; Apollos, the eloquent Alexandrian; Cephas (Peter), the original apostle; or even Christ, claiming superior spirituality (1 Corinthians 1:12). Paul rebukes them as "carnal" and "babes in Christ" (1 Corinthians 3:1, KJV), unable to digest the meat of God's Word. Their focus on personalities rather than on the gospel itself stunted their spiritual growth, leaving them stuck in spiritual infancy. Paul's solution to this immaturity and division is a powerful metaphor: the church as God's building, erected on a singular, unshakeable foundation.

> *"And I, brethren, could not speak unto you as unto spiritual, but as unto carnal, even as unto babes in Christ. I have fed you with milk, and not with meat: for hitherto ye were not able to bear it... For while one saith, I am of Paul; and another, I am of Apollos; are ye not carnal? Who then is Paul, and who is Apollos, but ministers by whom ye believed, even as the Lord gave to every man? I have planted, Apollos watered; but God gave the increase... Ye are God's husbandry, ye are God's building. According to the grace of God which is given unto me, as a wise masterbuilder, I have laid*

*the foundation, and another buildeth thereon. But let every man take heed how he buildeth thereupon. For other foundation can no man lay than that is laid, which is Jesus Christ. Now if any man build upon this foundation gold, silver, precious stones, wood, hay, stubble; Every man's work shall be made manifest: for the day shall declare it, because it shall be revealed by fire... Know ye not that ye are the temple of God, and that the Spirit of God dwelleth in you? If any man defile the temple of God, him shall God destroy; for the temple of God is holy, which temple ye are. Let no man deceive himself. If any man among you seemeth to be wise in this world, let him become a fool, that he may be wise... And ye are Christ's; and Christ is God's." (1 Corinthians 3:1–6, 9–13, 16–18, 23, KJV)*

# The Foundation: Christ and Christ Alone

Paul, a wise masterbuilder, declares a truth that stands for all time: "For other foundation can no man lay than that is laid, which is Jesus Christ" (1 Corinthians 3:11). This is not a suggestion; it is a divine command. No church built on the shifting sands of human wisdom, personality, or cultural relevance can withstand the coming judgment. The foundation is fixed and unchangeable. It is Christ crucified, a stumbling block to the proud and foolishness to the world, yet to us who are called, it is the power of God unto salvation (1 Corinthians 1:18).

The cross is the only foundation because it is God's only remedy for man's willful rebellion, which began in Eden. Adam's sin was not a stumble but a conscious act of rebellion, a choice to "be as gods" (Genesis 3:5). No human effort—no philosophy, no social justice reform, no self-help technique—can repair the broken relationship that began in Eden. Only the shed blood of a perfect sacrifice can atone for our sin and rebuild the bridge to God. The cross humbles all, as it reveals the depth of our sin and the immensity of God's grace, uniting every believer—rich or poor, wise or foolish—at the foot of the cross.

## The Temple: Built with Eternal Materials

Just as Solomon's temple was built with carefully chosen, precious materials—gold, silver, and dressed stones—so too is God's spiritual house built with "lively stones" (1 Peter 2:5, KJV). The question for every builder, whether a pastor or a church member, is what materials are you using? Paul identifies two types of materials: those that endure the fire, and those that are consumed by it.

On one hand, we have "gold, silver, precious stones" (1 Corinthians 3:12). The Greek phrase for "precious stones," λίθους τιμίους (*lithous timious*), refers not to jewels but to valuable, dressed building materials like polished marble or granite. These stones are the believers themselves, and they are the genuine, Christ-centered materials for God's spiritual house. This is the church built of people who will not be destroyed by the fire of trial. Gold is a metal refined by fire. Silver is precious and pure. These stones are hard, beautiful, and lasting. They are like the stones used to build Solomon's temple, which were quarried and dressed off-site so that "neither hammer nor axe nor any tool of iron was heard in the house while it was being built" (1 Kings 6:7, KJV). In the same way, the church is built of people who have been prepared for their place. As in a physical building, every stone is necessary, supporting and requiring every other stone for the structure to stand firm. On the other hand, we have "wood, hay, stubble" (1 Corinthians 3:12). These are the cheap substitutes. They may look impressive on the surface—a ministry built on charisma, a church member drawn by social connections, a gospel of entertainment or personal gain. They may give the illusion of growth, but when tribulation comes—when the fire of testing reveals all—they will be consumed. Wood burns, hay turns to ash, and stubble vanishes in the flame. These materials represent work done for selfish gain, for human praise, or from a heart not truly submitted to Christ.

Paul's imagery is vivid: each believer is a stone, dressed and placed by God. If one stone is missing, the structure weakens. The temple's beauty lies not in its outward appearance but in its unity and holiness. When people see the church, they should not marvel at the preacher or the program, but at the God who transforms lives. The church's strength is not in its numbers or charisma but in its commitment to Christ's gospel.

## The Danger of Self-Deception and the Fire of Testing

Paul's warning is a solemn call to self-examination: "Know ye not that ye are the temple of God, and that the Spirit of God dwelleth in you?" (1 Corinthians 3:16). This is a piercing question for every believer. Are we a genuine stone, fitted and purified by the Holy Spirit for God's glory? Or are we a piece of wood or hay, drawn to the outward show of the church but lacking the inward reality of Christ?

Many interpreters, including some of my respected colleagues, have traditionally viewed this passage (1 Corinthians 3:13-15) as a description of the Bema Seat, or Judgment Throne of Christ, where believers' works will be tested by fire at the end of the age. They see this "day" as a future, final judgment of our service.

However, when we read this passage in its immediate context, a different and equally compelling picture emerges. Paul is not suddenly jumping to a future eschatological event; he is continuing his urgent, practical instruction to the Corinthian church. He is

**See Appendix 1 For a more comprehensive discussion of "the day"**

addressing their present-day divisions and immaturity. I believe Paul is teaching that the "building materials" are not merely our works, but the very people we are building with, the members of the church themselves. And the "fire" is not a future bonfire in heaven, but the fires of tribulation, persecution, and false teaching that test a church's true foundation and its members' genuine faith.

We see this same imagery in 1 Peter 1:7, where the "trial of your faith" is likened to gold being "tried with fire." This is a present reality, not merely a future event. The "day" Paul speaks of can be understood as the time of testing that a church inevitably faces. A church built on such materials as personalities or social benefits will not withstand the trials of this present age, but will be consumed by them.

This interpretation of the "day revealed by fire" makes Paul's warning all the more urgent and practical for us today. It means we cannot wait for a future judgment to examine our motives or the quality of our church.

The test is not in the future; it is happening now. A fireproof church is not one that merely awaits a reward in heaven, but one that is actively being refined and strengthened on earth, standing firm against every fire that comes against it, because its foundation and its members are genuine.

## Conclusion: A Unified Temple for God's Glory

The church is God's temple, built on the foundation of Christ crucified and indwelt by His Spirit. Like Solomon's temple, adorned with gold, silver, and dressed stones, we must build with eternal materials to reflect God's glory.

Divisions, pride, and human wisdom weaken the structure, but the gospel unites us as a fireproof church, enduring trials and shining Christ's light. Let us examine our hearts, reject self-deception, and build faithfully, boasting only in the Lord who called us to His body. As we heed Paul's call to unity, we become a living temple, fitted together to glorify God in our communities and beyond.

# Application: Building a Fireproof Church

A fireproof church is united on the foundation of Christ, with believers fitted together as living stones. Here are five ways to apply this truth:

- **Examine Your Heart**: Reflect on 2 Corinthians 13:5 and ask, "Am I in the faith?" Is your presence in the church driven by Christ's call or by worldly motives like social connection, entertainment, or status? Ensure your heart rests in the gospel alone (Romans 10:9–10).

- **Build with Eternal Materials**: Serve with faith, obedience, and the gospel's truth, not fleeting motives like popularity or self-interest. As living stones, fit into God's design, supporting others in the body (1 Peter 2:5).

- **Reject Worldly Wisdom**: Lay aside pride in eloquence, trends, or human leaders. Embrace the "foolishness" of the gospel, trusting the Spirit to transform hearts (1 Corinthians 2:14). In a world driven by social media influencers and cultural fads, focus on Christ alone.

- **Grow in Spiritual Maturity**: Move beyond spiritual infancy by studying God's Word and allowing the Spirit to apply it. Like sandpaper, let Scripture

45

refine your heart, preparing you for God's work (Hebrews 5:12–14).

- **Support the Body**: As stones in God's temple, your presence strengthens the church. If you're absent or uncommitted, the structure weakens. Be present, serve faithfully, and support your brothers and sisters (Hebrews 10:24–25).

# Prayer

*Father, we thank You for calling us to unity as Your holy temple, a dwelling place for Your Spirit. Convict us if we are wood or stubble, and shape us into precious stones, fitted for Your glory. Help us reject worldly wisdom, grow in Your Word, and build together on the foundation of Christ alone. Make us a fireproof church that shines Your light in a divided world. In Jesus' name,*

*Amen.*

# 5

## Called to Faithfulness: Ministers and Stewards of Christ

### An Epilogue Before the Fire

In chapters 1–3, Paul exposed the danger of a church divided over personalities. The Corinthians had grown enamored with the style, charisma, and eloquence of preachers, losing sight of the message of the cross. He reminded them that the true test of a church is not its celebrity leaders, but whether it is built on Christ with gold, silver, and precious stones that can withstand the fire.

Now, in chapter 4, Paul brings this opening section to a close. Before turning to the painful subject of moral purity in chapter 5, he writes an epilogue—a sober reminder of what true Christian leadership looks like. Instead of pride and competition, Paul calls the church to see its leaders as servants of Christ and stewards of God's mysteries. This chapter explores what it means to be faithful stewards, judged not by human standards, but by the Lord Himself.

*Let a man so account of us, as of the ministers of Christ, and stewards of the mysteries of God. Moreover, it is required in stewards that a man be found faithful.*

*But with me it is a very small thing that I should be judged by you, or by man's judgment: yea, I judge not myself. For I know nothing by myself; yet am I not hereby justified: but he that judgeth me is the Lord. Therefore judge nothing before the time, until the Lord come, who both will bring to light the hidden things of darkness, and will make manifest the counsels of the hearts: and then shall every man have praise of God. And these things, brethren, I have in a figure transferred to myself and to Apollos for your sakes; that ye might learn in us not to think of men above that which is written, that no one of you be puffed up for one against another. For who maketh thee to differ from another? and what hast thou that thou didst not receive? now if thou didst receive it, why dost thou glory, as if thou hadst not received it?*

*Now ye are full, now ye are rich, ye have reigned as kings without us: and I would to God ye did reign, that we also might reign with you. For I think that God hath set forth us the apostles last, as it were appointed to death: for we are made a spectacle unto the world, and to angels, and to men. We are fools for Christ's sake, but ye are wise in Christ; we are weak, but ye are strong; ye are honourable, but we are despised. Even unto this present hour we both hunger, and thirst, and are naked, and are buffeted, and have no certain dwellingplace; And labour, working with our own hands: being reviled, we bless; being persecuted, we suffer it: Being defamed, we intreat: we are made as the filth of the world, and are the offscouring of all things unto this day. I write not these things to shame you, but as my beloved sons I warn you. (1 Corinthians 4:1-14, KJV)*

## Ministers and Stewards: Two Defining Roles

Paul begins: "Let a man so account of us, as of the ministers of Christ, and stewards of the mysteries of God" (1 Corinthians 4:1, KJV). Two words define the preacher's calling: minister and steward.

The word Paul uses for minister here is not the common term *diakonos* (deacon or servant), but a word drawn from the Athenian navy, originally describing an under-rower on a ship. Later, it came to mean a military adjutant—an officer who relayed a general's commands to the soldiers. An adjutant did not invent orders or act on personal authority; he simply conveyed the will of his commander. Paul is saying, "Do not think of us as brilliant strategists or charismatic leaders. Think of us as men who pass along the orders of Christ."

The second word, steward, pictures a household manager, like a butler who oversees resources that belong to another. The steward feeds the household, pays the servants, and manages affairs—but none of it belongs to him. Paul insists: "What I give you is not mine. I am entrusted with God's truth, and my task is to distribute it faithfully."

These two roles demolish pride. A minister is not a general but a messenger. A steward is not an owner but a manager. The task of every preacher is to equip the saints—to sharpen the sword of the Spirit, strengthen the shield of faith, and prepare God's people for battle. When a church makes celebrities out of ministers, it shifts the focus from Christ to His messengers, and the whole foundation begins to crack.

## Faithfulness, Not Eloquence

Paul continues: "Moreover it is required in stewards, that a man be found faithful" (1 Corinthians 4:2, KJV). Notice what is not required. Not eloquence. Not charisma. Not dazzling intellect. Faithfulness.

The Corinthians had judged Paul for his unimpressive delivery. "His letters are weighty and strong," they said, "but his bodily presence is weak, and his speech contemptible" (2 Corinthians 10:10). Paul shrugs off their critiques. Human opinion is not the measure of a steward; only the Master's judgment counts.

Paul writes, "With me it is a very small thing that I should be judged by you, or of man's judgment: yea, I judge not mine own self... but he that judgeth me is the Lord" (1 Corinthians 4:3–4, KJV). Faithfulness cannot be measured by style, delivery, or outward success. It is measured by whether the steward has faithfully transmitted what the Lord entrusted.

Here is encouragement for every Christian. You may not be eloquent, gifted, or outwardly impressive. But God is not asking for brilliance—He is asking for faithfulness. A fireproof church is built not on charisma but on consistent obedience.

## Judged by the Lord Alone

Paul warns against premature judgment: "Therefore judge nothing before the time, until the Lord come" (1 Corinthians 4:5, KJV). Life cannot be evaluated mid-race. True assessment comes only at the bema seat of Christ, when He will bring to light the hidden things of the heart.

This judgment is not about condemning sin—Christ bore that judgment at the cross. Rather, it is about testing motives. Did we serve for applause or for Christ? Did we preach to gain followers, or to exalt the Lord? At that day, Paul promises, "then shall every man have praise of God." What a staggering thought —that Christ will find something to commend in every believer's life.

The goal, then, is not to earn man's praise but to live so that the Lord will have much to say on that day: "Well done, thou good and faithful servant." A fireproof church is made up of men and women who labor for that commendation alone.

## Staying Within What Is Written

Paul applies this lesson to himself and Apollos, saying he has used them as examples "that ye might learn in us not to think of men above that which is written" (1 Corinthians 4:6, KJV). Some in Corinth were exalting teachers who went beyond Scripture with novel ideas. Paul draws a line: stay within the bounds of the Word.

The Word of God is sufficient, complete, and authoritative. To exalt human wisdom above it is to invite pride, rivalry, and heresy. A fireproof church resists the temptation to chase novelty or personalities. It is anchored in what is written.

## Apostolic Suffering and Fatherly Care

The Corinthians were puffed up, proud of their gifts and knowledge. Paul responds with biting irony: "Now ye are full, now ye are rich, ye have reigned as kings without us" (1 Corinthians 4:8, KJV). By contrast, the apostles were despised, hungry, homeless, and treated as the "offscouring of all things" (v. 13).

Would anyone endure such suffering for a lie? The apostles' poverty and persecution proved the sincerity of their message. They were "fools for Christ's sake" (v. 10), spectacles before the world, displaying the power of the cross not in ease but in endurance.

Yet Paul softens his tone: "I write not these things to shame you, but as my beloved sons I warn you" (v. 14). They may have ten thousand instructors, but Paul alone was their father in the gospel. Like a spiritual parent, he pleads: "Be ye followers of me" (v. 16). He sends Timothy to remind them not only of his teaching, but of his ways in Christ. True discipleship is more than words; it is a life lived out before others.

## The Kingdom in Power, Not Words

Paul closes with a challenge: "The kingdom of God is not in word, but in power" (v. 20). Eloquence and showmanship are worthless without the transforming power of the gospel. Some in Corinth boasted as though Paul would never return, but he warns them:

he will come, and when he does, he will test not their speech but their power.

The gospel's power is not measured in rhetoric but in changed lives. A fireproof church is not defined by polished sermons or polished appearances, but by the Spirit's power to save, sanctify, and sustain. That is the measure of true ministry.

## Conclusion: Faithful Stewards of Christ

Chapter 4 closes Paul's appeal against division with a portrait of true leadership. Ministers are not celebrities but servants. Stewards are not innovators but faithful managers of Christ's mysteries. Apostles suffered, not to shame the church, but to model the way of the cross. And in the end, every steward will give account to the Lord.

A fireproof church is one that prizes faithfulness over flair, substance over style, the power of the gospel over the polish of men. May we be such a church—faithful stewards, awaiting the commendation of our Lord.

# Application: Building a Faithful Church

From Paul's epilogue, we draw several lessons for building a fireproof church:

- **See Ministers Rightly**: Pastors are not generals but messengers, not masters but stewards. Exalt Christ, not His servants.

- **Value Faithfulness Above Talent**: God rewards consistency, not charisma. Judge ministry by faithfulness to the Word.

- **Wait for the Lord's Commendation**: Resist premature judgments—yours or others'. Live for the "Well done" of Christ.

- **Stay Within Scripture**: Do not exalt human wisdom above what is written. Let God's Word be the boundary and anchor.

- **Follow Godly Examples**: Seek leaders who live what they preach. Learn not just from their words but from their walk.

- **Rely on the Gospel's Power**: The kingdom is not in empty speech but in lives transformed by Christ's Spirit.

## Prayer

*Father, we thank You for entrusting us with the mysteries of Christ. Teach us to be faithful stewards, not seeking man's praise but Yours alone. Keep us within the bounds of Your Word, and may the power of the gospel shape our lives. In Jesus' name,*

*Amen.*

# 6

## Called to Purity: Cleansing the Body of Christ

### A Holy Church in a Sinful World

The Corinthian church, birthed in the furnace of a city steeped in immorality and pride, faced a critical test: could it remain a holy people in the midst of Corinth's debauchery? In 1 Corinthians 5, Paul confronts a shocking scandal—a man living in open sin, celebrated by the church for its tolerance. This was not just a personal failing but a betrayal of their calling as God's holy people. Paul's response is both a rebuke and a call to action: remove the sin, purify the body, and celebrate the Passover with the unleavened bread of sincerity and truth. For a church to be fireproof, it must reject the leaven of sin, embrace loving discipline, and live as a redeemed community transformed by Christ, our Passover Lamb.

This chapter explores 1 Corinthians 5, where Paul addresses the Corinthians' pride in tolerating sin, their misunderstanding of Christian freedom, and their failure to protect the body of Christ. We will examine the cultural context of Corinth's permissive morality, the biblical mandate for church discipline, and the hope of redemption through Christ's sacrifice. Just as the Corinthians were tempted to mirror their city's values, today's church faces pressure to embrace cultural norms over biblical holiness. Paul's words challenge us to be a fireproof church: one that lovingly corrects sin, guards its purity, and glorifies God as a holy, unified body.

> *It is reported commonly that there is fornication among you, and such fornication as is not so much as named among the Gentiles, that one should have his father's wife. And ye are puffed up, and have not rather mourned, that he that hath done this deed might be taken away from among you. For I verily, as absent in body, but present in spirit, have judged already, as though I were present, concerning him that hath so done this deed, in the name of our Lord Jesus Christ, when ye are gathered together, and my spirit, with the power of our Lord Jesus Christ, to deliver such an one unto Satan for the destruction of the flesh, that the spirit may be saved in the day of the Lord Jesus.*

*Your glorying is not good. Know ye not that a little leaven leaveneth the whole lump? Purge out therefore the old leaven, that ye may be a new lump, as ye are unleavened. For even Christ our Passover is sacrificed for us: Therefore let us keep the feast, not with old leaven, neither with the leaven of malice and wickedness; but with the unleavened bread of sincerity and truth. I wrote unto you in an epistle not to company with fornicators: Yet not altogether with the fornicators of this world, or with the covetous, or extortioners, or with idolaters; for then must ye needs go out of the world. But now I have written unto you not to keep company, if any man that is called a brother be a fornicator, or covetous, or an idolator, or a railer, or a drunkard, or an extortioner; with such an one no not to eat. For what have I to do to judge them also that are without? Do not ye judge them that are within? But them that are without God judgeth. Therefore put away from among yourselves that wicked person. (1 Corinthians 5, KJV)*

## The Scandal of Tolerated Sin: A Corrupted Witness

Paul opens 1 Corinthians 5 with a tone of disbelief: "It is actually reported that sexual immorality exists among you, the kind of immorality that is not permitted even among the Gentiles, so that someone is living with his father's wife. And you are proud!" (1 Corinthians 5:1–2, KJV). The sin—a man living with his father's wife, likely his stepmother—was so egregious that even Corinth's pagan society, notorious for its temple prostitutes and moral laxity, would have condemned it. Yet, the Corinthian church, instead of mourning, was celebrating this man's sin, boasting in their "tolerance" and "acceptance." Paul is shocked: "Should you not have been deeply sorrowful instead and have removed the one who did this from among you?" (1 Corinthians 5:2, KJV).

This scandal reflects the Corinthian culture we explored in Chapter 1. Corinth, a city rebuilt as a Roman colony, thrived on wealth, competition, and moral permissiveness. The temple of Aphrodite, with its sacred prostitutes, symbolized a society where sexual immorality was normalized, even celebrated. The Corinthians brought this mindset into the church, adopting a "big tent" mentality: "Come as you are, live as you want, and Christ will forgive everything." Paul's rebuke echoes through the centuries to our 21st-century churches, where tolerance is often prized over holiness. How many congregations today, eager to be welcoming, shy away from confronting sin, saying, "Just come, and it's okay—whatever's going on, we accept you"? While the church is indeed the most welcoming place in the world—open to all at the foot of the cross—it is also an exclusive body of redeemed sinners, called to live in holiness.

Paul's outrage is not rooted in self-righteousness but in love for the church and the sinner. He writes, "Your boasting is not good. Do you not know that a little yeast affects the whole batch of dough?" (1 Corinthians 5:6, KJV). Sin, like yeast, spreads, corrupting the entire body. The Corinthians' pride in their non-judgmental attitude was not loving; it was enabling destruction. As Paul explains, sin doesn't just harm the individual—it sickens the whole church. "If one part of the body has an illness, then the whole body is sick." This mirrors the Old Testament example of Achan, whose sin in Joshua 7 brought defeat to Israel until it was addressed. A fireproof church cannot tolerate sin within its ranks, for it undermines the witness of Christ's holiness and harms the sinner's soul.

## The Call to Discipline: Loving Correction

Paul's solution is stark: "Remove the evil person from among you" (1 Corinthians 5:13, KJV). This echoes Deuteronomy's command to purge evil from Israel (Deuteronomy 17:7), emphasizing the seriousness of sin in God's people. But this call to church discipline is not about judgmentalism or exclusion for exclusion's sake. Paul's motivation is love—for the sinner, the church, and Christ's glory. He instructs, "When you gather together in the name of our Lord Jesus and I am with you in spirit, along with the power of our Lord Jesus, hand this man over to Satan for the destruction of the flesh, so that his spirit may be saved in the day of the Lord" (1 Corinthians 5:4–5, KJV).

The phrase "hand this man over to Satan" is jarring, but it's not about eternal condemnation. If the man is a true believer, his salvation is secure, as Paul notes that his spirit may be saved. Rather, this is about removing him from the protective fellowship of the church, allowing him to face the consequences of his sin in the world—described as Satan's domain. Paul explains, "Sin destroys the body." Living in unrepentant sin leads to a downward spiral, physically and spiritually, as the sinner reaps the consequences of their choices. The goal is not punishment but restoration: that the man might repent and return, as we learn in 2 Corinthians 2:5–11, where Paul indicates that this man did repent and was restored to fellowship.

Church discipline, as Paul outlines, follows Jesus' teaching in Matthew 18:15–17: confront the sin privately, then with witnesses, and finally before the church. If the sinner refuses to repent, the church must act, not out of pride or superiority, but out of love, saying, "We cannot continue to say that what you're doing is okay, because we know the harm it's doing to you." This is not about being "too good" for the sinner but about protecting the body and calling the individual to repentance. As Paul notes, "By accepting his sin, they were not loving him. The loving thing to do was to put him out of the fellowship so that he could have the room to repent."

This challenges our modern sensibilities. Discipline sounds harsh, intolerant, or judgmental in a culture that equates love with unconditional affirmation. Yet, Paul's teaching is clear: true love warns of sin's consequences. Just as a parent disciplines a child to protect them from harm, the church disciplines to protect its members and its witness. A fireproof church practices loving discipline, not to exclude but to restore, ensuring that the body remains pure and its testimony strong.

## Christ, Our Passover Lamb: A Call to Purity

Paul roots his call to holiness in the imagery of the Passover: "Clean out the old yeast so that you may be a new batch of dough—you are, in fact, without yeast. For Christ our Passover Lamb has been sacrificed. So then, let us celebrate the festival, not with the old yeast, the yeast of vice and evil, but with the bread without yeast, the bread of sincerity and truth" (1 Corinthians 5:7–8, KJV). This powerful metaphor draws from the Old Testament, where Israel was commanded to remove all leaven from their homes before the Passover (Exodus 12:15). Leaven, a symbol of sin, had to be purged to prepare for the sacrifice of the Passover lamb, which delivered them from death.

Paul declares that Christ is our Passover Lamb, sacrificed to deliver us from sin's penalty. The Corinthians, as believers, are "without yeast"—redeemed and made holy by Christ's blood. Yet, they were allowing the "old yeast" of sin to remain, corrupting the body. Paul urges them to live out their identity as a holy people, celebrating the "festival" of their redemption with sincerity and truth. The Greek word for sincerity, *eilikrineia*, means to be examined in the sunlight, implying transparency and integrity. A fireproof church lives openly before God, with nothing to hide, reflecting the purity of Christ.

The Feast of Unleavened Bread, which followed the Passover, reminded Israel of their hasty departure from Egypt, eating unleavened bread because they had no time to let dough rise (Exodus 12:34). Paul applies this to the church: "We too are on a journey. We don't have time to let the leaven rise in our lives and in our church. We are headed to a promised land, and we have a purpose to move on." Like the Israelites, we are a people on a mission, called to lay aside "every weight, and the sin which doth so easily beset us" (Hebrews 12:1, KJV) and run the race toward Christ. A fireproof church rejects the leaven of sin, living with urgency and purpose for God's glory.

## Judging Within, Not Without: A Higher Standard

Paul clarifies a misunderstanding from his earlier "lost letter" (referenced in 1 Corinthians 5:9): "I wrote you in my letter not to associate with sexually immoral people. In no way did I mean the immoral people of this world, or the greedy, or swindlers, or idolaters, since you would then have to go out of the world" (1 Corinthians 5:9–10, KJV). The Corinthians had misinterpreted Paul's instruction, thinking they should shun sinners in the world. Paul corrects them: "But now I am writing to you not to associate with anyone who calls himself a Christian who is sexually immoral, or greedy, or an idolater, or verbally abusive, or a drunkard, or a swindler—do not even eat with such a person" (1 Corinthians 5:11, KJV).

This distinction is crucial. The church is not called to judge the world—Jesus said the world is "condemned already" (John 3:18, KJV). Our mission is to reach sinners with the gospel, not to condemn them. But within the church, we hold one another to a higher standard, not out of pride or self-righteousness, but out of love. Paul lists sins—sexual immorality, greed, idolatry, verbal abuse, drunkenness, swindling—that are incompatible with a life surrendered to Christ.

These are not just "big" sins but include everyday behaviors like greed and verbal abuse, reminding us that all sin disrupts the body's holiness.

The command "do not even eat with such a person" underscores the seriousness of unrepentant sin within the church. In Corinth, sharing a meal was a sign of fellowship, so to withhold it was a visible act of discipline, signaling that the sinner's behavior was unacceptable. This is not about snobbery but about calling one another to holiness. Paul is calling us to love one another so that we can draw one another to holiness for the good of each other. A fireproof church holds its members accountable, not to exclude but to restore them to fellowship with Christ and His body.

## The Power of Fellowship: Protection in the Body

Paul's call to remove the sinner highlights the vital role of church fellowship. He warns that living outside the church is to be "handed over to Satan" (1 Corinthians 5:5, KJV), a terrifying reality. The church is a place of protection, grace, and strength, where believers share life and grow in holiness together. Paul's words show us that church membership, church participation, is vital to the Christian. There is a protection, a grace, a strength, a shared life within the body of Christ that you do not participate in if you do not regularly participate with that body. To be removed from this fellowship is to be exposed to the destructive consequences of sin, as "sin destroys the body."

This truth challenges our modern individualism. Many believers today claim faith in Christ but avoid regular church involvement, thinking they can "go it alone." Paul's warning is clear: outside the fellowship of the church, we place ourselves in danger, vulnerable to the enemy's influence. The restoration of the disciplined man in 2 Corinthians shows the power of this process—discipline led to repentance, and the church welcomed him back. A fireproof church is a community that protects its members through loving accountability, ensuring that each part of the body remains healthy and whole.

## Conclusion: A Pure and Holy Body

The Corinthian church, like ours, was called to be a fireproof church—pure, united, and set apart for God's glory. In a city that celebrated sin, they were to shine as a holy people, cleansed by Christ's sacrifice. Paul's words in 1 Corinthians 5 challenge us to reject the leaven of sin, practice loving discipline, and live as a community transformed by our Passover Lamb. As members of Christ's body, we are not our own but His, called to live with sincerity and truth. Let us build a church that glorifies God, protects its members, and shines as a beacon of holiness in a sinful world.

# Application: Building a Fireproof Church

A fireproof church is pure, united, and committed to Christ's holiness. Here are four ways to apply 1 Corinthians 5:

- **Reject Tolerated Sin:** Like yeast, sin spreads, corrupting the body. Mourn over sin in the church, not with pride or tolerance, but with a heart for restoration. Examine your own life for any "leaven" that hinders your walk with Christ.

- **Practice Loving Discipline:** Follow the biblical model of Matthew 18, confronting sin privately, with witnesses, and, if necessary, before the church. Discipline is not judgmentalism but an act of love, aiming to restore the sinner to fellowship.

- **Live as Unleavened Bread:** As those redeemed by Christ, our Passover Lamb, live with sincerity and truth, transparent before God and others. Lay aside sin and run the race toward the promised land with urgency.

- **Value Church Fellowship:** Commit to regular participation in the body of Christ. The church is a place of protection and growth, where we hold one another accountable and draw closer to Christ together.

# Prayer

*Father, we thank You for calling us to be Your holy people, redeemed by Christ, our Passover Lamb. Help us to reject sin, practice loving discipline, and live with sincerity and truth. Build us into a fireproof church that glorifies You. In Jesus' name,*

*Amen.*

# 7

## Called to Holiness: The Body as God's Temple

### A Call to Purity in a Corrupt World

The Corinthian church, planted in the furnace of a pagan city, faced a crucible of moral and relational challenges. In 1 Corinthians 6, Paul confronts a church entangled in lawsuits, defrauding one another, and succumbing to the sexual immorality that defined their city. These were not mere personal failings but a betrayal of their calling as a holy people, a fireproof church set apart for God's glory.

Paul's words in this chapter are a clarion call to reject the world's values, to resolve disputes within the body of Christ, and to honor God with their bodies as temples of the Holy Spirit. For today's church, surrounded by a culture that normalizes sin and division, this passage offers a blueprint for holiness, unity, and a witness that endures the fires of a fallen world.

This chapter delves into 1 Corinthians 6, exploring how Paul addresses the Corinthians' failure to live as a sanctified community. We will examine the scandal of Christians taking each other to court, the sobering warning about the unrighteous, and the radical truth that our bodies belong to God. Through Paul's teaching, we will uncover the principles of a fireproof church: one that settles disputes in love, flees from sin, and glorifies God in body, mind, and soul. Just as Corinth's culture of pride and immorality threatened to fracture the church, our modern world tempts us to conform. Yet, Paul's message remains clear: we are called to be saints, a holy people who reflect Christ's purity in a corrupt world.

*Dare any of you, having a matter against another, go to law before the unjust, and not before the saints? Do ye not know that the saints shall judge the world? And if the world shall be judged by you, are ye unworthy to judge the smallest matters? Know ye not that we shall judge angels? How much more things that pertain to this life? If then ye have judgments of things pertaining to this life, set them to judge who are least esteemed in the church. I speak to your shame. Is it so, that there is not a wise man among you? No, not one that shall be able to judge between his brethren? But brother goeth to law with brother, and that before the unbelievers. Now therefore*

there is utterly a fault among you, because ye
go to law one with another. Why do ye not
rather take wrong? Why do ye not rather suffer
yourselves to be defrauded? Nay, ye do wrong,
and defraud, and that your brethren. Know ye
not that the unrighteous shall not inherit the
kingdom of God? Be not deceived: neither
fornicators, nor idolaters, nor adulterers, nor
effeminate, nor abusers of themselves with
mankind, nor thieves, nor covetous, nor
drunkards, nor revilers, nor extortioners, shall
inherit the kingdom of God. And such were
some of you: but ye are washed, but ye are
sanctified, but ye are justified in the name of
the Lord Jesus, and by the Spirit of our God. All
things are lawful unto me, but all things are not
expedient: all things are lawful for me, but I will
not be brought under the power of any. Meats
for the belly, and the belly for meats: but God
shall destroy both it and them. Now the body is
not for fornication, but for the Lord; and the
Lord for the body. And God hath both raised up
the Lord, and will also raise up us by his own
power. Know ye not that your bodies are the
members of Christ? Shall I then take the
members of Christ, and make them the
members of an harlot? God forbid. What?
Know ye not that he which is joined to an harlot
is one body? For two, saith he, shall be one
flesh. But he that is joined unto the Lord is one

*spirit. Flee fornication. Every sin that a man doeth is without the body; but he that committeth fornication sinneth against his own body. What? Know ye not that your body is the temple of the Holy Ghost which is in you, which ye have of God, and ye are not your own? For ye are bought with a price: therefore glorify God in your body, and in your spirit, which are God's. (1 Corinthians 6, KJV)*

## The Scandal of Lawsuits: A Defeated Witness

Paul begins 1 Corinthians 6 with a shocking rebuke: "When one of you has a legal dispute with another, does he dare go to court before the unrighteous rather than before the saints?" (1 Corinthians 6:1, KJV).

The Corinthians, steeped in their city's competitive culture, were dragging their disputes before pagan courts, airing their grievances before unbelievers. This was not just a practical misstep; it was a spiritual defeat. Paul declares, "The fact that you have lawsuits among yourselves demonstrates that you have already been defeated" (1 Corinthians 6:7, KJV). By taking their quarrels to worldly judges, they were tearing apart the body of Christ publicly, tarnishing their witness, and dishonoring their Lord.

Corinth's culture, as we explored in Chapter 1, was obsessed with status, reputation, and one-upmanship. The Isthmian Games, the city's bustling trade, and its social hierarchy fueled a mindset of self-promotion and pride.

The Corinthians brought this mindset into the church, defrauding and cheating one another, then seeking justice in courts known for corruption. Paul is appalled: "I say this to your shame. Is there no one among you wise enough to settle disputes between fellow Christians?" (1 Corinthians 6:5, KJV). He reminds them of their future role: "Do you not know that the saints will judge the world? ... Do you not know that we will judge angels?" (1 Corinthians 6:2–3, KJV). If they are destined to rule with Christ in eternity, how can they lack the wisdom to resolve "trivial suits" within the church?

This issue resonates with churches today. How often do we see believers, hurt or wronged, turn to the world's systems for justice rather than seeking reconciliation within the body? Whether it's a public dispute on social media or a legal battle over property, the result is the same: the name of Christ is dragged through the mud. Paul's solution is radical: "Why not rather be wronged? Why not rather be cheated?" (1 Corinthians 6:7, KJV). Better to suffer loss than to let the world witness a fractured church. A fireproof church prioritizes Christ's reputation over personal gain, choosing love over lawsuits and unity over victory in court.

## The Church as Arbiter: Wisdom in the Body

Paul's challenge to the Corinthians is not just to avoid pagan courts but to find wisdom within the church. He asks, "Is there no one among you wise enough to settle disputes between fellow Christians?" (1 Corinthians 6:5, KJV). This is a call to lean on the Holy Spirit's guidance within the body of Christ. The church, as the *ekklēsia*—a called-out assembly—has the resources to resolve conflicts through godly counsel. Paul isn't advocating for formal church courts, as some denominations practice, but for a community approach: "Just get together with another church member and say, 'Here, will you listen to both sides and help guide us through this dispute, help us to find agreement?'" Sometimes, we are so caught up in our own feelings and reactions that we cannot see the other side. A godly brother or sister, filled with the Spirit, can mediate with love and wisdom, pointing both parties toward God's will.

This principle challenges our modern individualism. In Corinth, as in our world, people were quick to assert their rights: "He cheated me more than I cheated him!" Paul counters that the church is one body, and harming one another harms Christ. The Roman courts, like many modern legal systems, were corrupt, favoring the wealthy or well-connected. Paul notes, "You'll take it before people who have no standing in the church" (1 Corinthians 6:4, KJV). Even the least member of the church, filled with the Holy Spirit, is better equipped to judge disputes than a worldly court. This echoes Jesus' teaching in Matthew 18:15–17, where disputes are resolved within the church, escalating only if necessary, but always with the goal of restoration, not retribution.

Imagine the witness of a church that handles conflict this way—quietly, lovingly, within the body. Instead of public feuds that fuel gossip, a fireproof church demonstrates Christ's love by resolving disputes in a way that glorifies God. This requires humility, a willingness to listen, and a commitment to the body over self. As Paul says, "What is more important: your stuff or your Lord? What is more important: your pride or the reputation of your church in the community?" A fireproof church chooses Christ over possessions, unity over personal vindication.

## The Unrighteous and the Kingdom: A Sobering Warning

Paul's rebuke deepens as he addresses the root of their disputes: a failure to live as a holy people. He writes, "Do you not know that the unrighteous will not inherit the kingdom of God? Do not be deceived: the sexually immoral, idolaters, adulterers, passive homosexual partners, practicing homosexuals, thieves, the greedy, drunkards, the verbally abusive, and swindlers will not inherit the kingdom of God" (1 Corinthians 6:9–10, KJV). This list is not just a catalog of sins but a mirror held up to the Corinthians' lives. Their lawsuits stemmed from greed, cheating, and pride—sins that characterized the unrighteous, not the saints.

This warning is sobering. Paul is addressing a "mixed flock," a church with genuine believers and those who merely profess faith. He challenges them to examine themselves: "If I am not demonstrating the lordship of Christ in my life, if my priorities are not Christ's priorities, if my love is not Christ's love, if my choices are not Christ's choices, then am I a disciple of Christ?" The unrighteous, whose lives are defined by these sins, will not inherit God's kingdom. This is not about losing salvation but about whether one has truly surrendered to Christ. As Jesus said, "By their fruits ye shall know them" (Matthew 7:20, KJV).

## What do we produce—love, peace, and joy, or stress, anxiety, and frustration?

Paul's list of sins is striking because it includes not only "big" sins like sexual immorality and idolatry but also "everyday" sins like greed and verbal abuse. In

77

Corinth, as in our world, we tend to rank sins: "That sin is horrible; mine is okay." But Paul places greed and verbal abuse alongside adultery and theft, reminding us that all sin separates us from God's holiness. The Corinthians' cheating and lawsuits were as much a betrayal of their calling as any sexual sin. A fireproof church examines its fruit, asking, "Does my life reflect Christ's righteousness, or am I living for myself?"

Yet, Paul offers hope: "Some of you once lived this way, but you were washed, you were sanctified, you were justified in the name of the Lord Jesus Christ and by the Spirit of our God" (1 Corinthians 6:11, KJV). This is the gospel's power. No sin is beyond God's grace. The Corinthians, once steeped in Corinth's debauchery, were transformed by Christ's blood. They were washed—cleansed from sin's stain; sanctified—set apart for God's use; and justified— clothed in Christ's righteousness. This is the foundation of a fireproof church: not our perfection, but Christ's finished work.

## The Body as God's Temple: A Call to Purity

Paul shifts from disputes to a deeper issue: the misuse of the body. He writes, "All things are lawful for me, but not everything is beneficial. All things are lawful for me, but I will not be controlled by anything"

(1 Corinthians 6:12, KJV). Some Corinthians, misunderstanding their freedom in Christ, justified sinful behavior, particularly sexual immorality. They argued, "Food is for the stomach and the stomach for food" (1 Corinthians 6:13, KJV), implying that bodily desires, like eating or sex, were neutral and could be indulged without consequence. Paul refutes this: "The body is not for sexual immorality but for the Lord, and the Lord for the body" (1 Corinthians 6:13, KJV).

This leads to a profound truth: "Do you not know that your body is the temple of the Holy Spirit who is in you, whom you have from God, and you are not your own? For you were bought at a price; therefore glorify God with your body" (1 Corinthians 6:19–20, KJV). In Chapter 1, we saw the church as God's temple, a community where God dwells.

Now, Paul declares that each believer's body is a temple, indwelt by the Holy Spirit. This is a radical claim. In Corinth, temples were places of idolatry and immorality, like the temple of Aphrodite with its sacred prostitutes. Paul redefines the body as sacred, purchased by Christ's blood, and meant to glorify God.

Sexual sin, Paul warns, is uniquely damaging: "Every sin a person commits is outside the body, but the immoral person sins against his own body" (1 Corinthians 6:18, KJV). Unlike other sins, sexual immorality unites the body—God's temple—with sin, desecrating what belongs to Christ. Paul's command is urgent: "Flee sexual immorality" (1 Corinthians 6:18, KJV). This echoes Joseph's flight from Potiphar's wife (Genesis 39:12), a model of resisting temptation. In Corinth's hyper-sexualized culture, where prostitution was normalized, this was a countercultural call to purity.

Paul's teaching applies to our world, where sexual sin is celebrated, and fidelity is mocked. Modern psychology, catching up to Scripture, confirms that multiple sexual partners diminish happiness and harm one's ability to form stable relationships. Paul's wisdom, rooted in God's design, shows that monogamous, faithful marriage is the path to joy. A fireproof church flees from sexual sin, recognizing that our bodies are not our own but belong to Christ, purchased at the infinite price of His blood.

## The Power to Overcome: Christ's Resurrection

Paul doesn't leave the Corinthians with a list of rules but with hope: "Now God indeed raised the Lord, and He will raise us by His power" (1 Corinthians 6:14, KJV). The same God who raised Jesus from the dead empowers believers to overcome sin. No 12-step program or human effort can free us from fleshly desires; only the Holy Spirit, working through God's Word, can transform us. Paul's call to fill ourselves with Scripture, rather than the "junk of the world," equips us to live as temples of God.

This resurrection power is the heart of a fireproof church. The Corinthians, addicted to sin, needed to hear that God's strength was greater than their weakness. So do we. Whether it's sexual temptation, greed, or the pride that fuels lawsuits, the Spirit enables us to say, "I will not be controlled by anything" (1 Corinthians 6:12, KJV). This freedom is not license to sin but liberation to live for Christ, glorifying Him in every aspect of life.

## Conclusion: A Holy Temple

The Corinthian church, like ours, was called to be a fireproof church—holy, united, and set apart for God's glory. In a city of immorality and pride, they were to shine as saints, reflecting Christ's righteousness. Paul's words in 1 Corinthians 6 challenge us to reject worldly disputes, flee from sin, and honor God with our bodies. As temples of the Holy Spirit, we are not our own but Christ's, purchased at the infinite price of His blood. Let us live as a unified, holy body, glorifying Him in a world that desperately needs His light.

# Application: Building a Fireproof Church

A fireproof church is holy, united, and devoted to glorifying God. Here are four ways to apply 1 Corinthians 6:

- **Resolve Disputes in Love**: Instead of taking grievances to the world, seek godly counsel within the church. Be willing to be wronged rather than dishonor Christ's name. Ask, "What is more important: my stuff or my Lord?"

- **Examine Your Fruit**: Are you producing love, peace, and joy, or stress and division? Test your life against Paul's warning: the unrighteous will not inherit God's kingdom. Surrender to Christ's lordship daily.

- **Flee from Sin**: Recognize that your body is God's temple, purchased by Christ's blood. Flee sexual immorality and any sin that controls you, trusting the Spirit's power to overcome.

- **Glorify God in Your Body**: Live as one bought at a price, honoring God in body, mind, and soul. Reject the world's lie that you can separate your spiritual life from your physical choices.

# Prayer

*Father, we thank You for calling us to be Your holy people, temples of Your Spirit. Help us to resolve disputes in love, flee from sin, and glorify You with our bodies. Build us into a fireproof church that shines for You. In Jesus' name,*

*Amen.*

# 8

## Called to Contentment: Living Lightly in a Passing World

### Introduction: A Church Anchored in Eternity

The Corinthian church, planted in a city of wealth, ambition, and fleeting pleasures, faced a profound challenge: how to live as God's holy people in a world that is passing away. In 1 Corinthians 7, Paul addresses practical questions about marriage, singleness, and life circumstances, offering wisdom for a church navigating a culture obsessed with status and self-fulfillment. His counsel is not a rigid rulebook but a call to contentment, urging believers to hold earthly relationships and circumstances lightly in light of eternity. For a church to be fireproof, it must prioritize Christ above all, finding peace in God's calling and living with an eternal perspective in a temporary world.

This chapter explores 1 Corinthians 7, where Paul responds to the Corinthians' questions about marriage, divorce, and their station in life. We will examine the cultural pressures of Corinth that shaped their concerns, Paul's balanced teaching on relationships, and the transformative truth that our ultimate allegiance is to Christ. In a world that tempts us to cling to possessions, relationships, or status, Paul's words challenge us to live as pilgrims, anchored in eternity. A fireproof church is one that embraces God's calling, serves Him faithfully in every circumstance, and prepares for the day when this world's form passes away.

> *Now concerning the things whereof ye wrote unto me: It is good for a man not to touch a woman. Nevertheless, to avoid fornication, let every man have his own wife, and let every woman have her own husband. Let the husband render unto the wife due benevolence: and likewise also the wife unto the husband. The wife hath not power of her own body, but the husband: and likewise also the husband hath not power of his own body, but the wife. Defraud ye not one the other, except it be with consent for a time, that ye may give yourselves to fasting and prayer; and come together again, that Satan tempt you not for your incontinency. But I speak this by permission, and not of commandment. For I would that all men were even as I myself. But every man hath his proper gift of God, one after this manner, and another after that. I say therefore to the unmarried and widows, it is*

*good for them if they abide even as I. But if they cannot contain, let them marry: for it is better to marry than to burn. (1 Corinthians 7:1-9, KJV)*

## The Corinthian Questions: Marriage and Singleness

Paul begins 1 Corinthians 7 with a response to the Corinthians' letter: "Now concerning the things whereof ye wrote unto me: It is good for a man not to touch a woman" (1 Corinthians 7:1, KJV). While we don't have the Corinthians' exact questions, Paul's answers suggest they were grappling with whether marriage was desirable or if singleness was spiritually superior, and whether believers should divorce unbelieving spouses. These questions reflect the cultural and spiritual tensions in Corinth, a city where sexual immorality was rampant, as seen in Chapters 3 and 4, and where social status and personal ambition dominated.

Corinth's culture, as we explored in Chapter 1, was shaped by its wealth, trade, and Roman hierarchy. Marriage, in this context, was often a strategic alliance for social or economic gain, not a sacred covenant. At the same time, some in the church, influenced by ascetic philosophies or fears of impending hardship, wondered if abstaining from marriage was a higher calling. Paul's response is both practical and profound, addressing their concerns while redirecting their focus to God's eternal purposes.

Paul acknowledges, "It is good for a man not to touch a woman" (1 Corinthians 7:1, KJV), affirming that singleness can be a gift for devoted service to God. Yet, he quickly counters the dangers of immorality: "Nevertheless, to avoid fornication, let every man have his own wife, and let every woman have her own husband" (1 Corinthians 7:2, KJV).

Marriage is God's design to protect against the sexual sin that pervaded Corinth, a city infamous for its temple of Aphrodite. Paul emphasizes mutual responsibility: "Let the husband render unto the wife due benevolence: and likewise also the wife unto the husband. The wife hath not power of her own body, but the husband: and likewise also the husband hath not power of his own body, but the wife" (1 Corinthians 7:3–4, KJV). This mutual submission was revolutionary in a culture where men held dominant power, underscoring that marriage is a partnership of self-giving love.

Paul advises couples not to deprive one another, except by mutual consent for prayer, to avoid temptation: "Defraud ye not one the other, except it be with consent for a time, that ye may give yourselves to fasting and prayer; and come together again, that Satan tempt you not for your incontinency" (1

Corinthians 7:5, KJV). This balance—honoring marriage while allowing space for spiritual devotion—shows Paul's pastoral heart. A fireproof church values marriage as God's gift but keeps it in perspective, ensuring that Christ remains first.

## Singleness as a Gift: Paul's Personal Perspective

Paul offers his personal perspective: "I say therefore to the unmarried and widows, It is good for them if they abide even as I. But if they cannot contain, let them marry: for it is better to marry than to burn" (1 Corinthians 7:8–9, KJV). As a widower, Paul had found contentment in singleness, dedicating himself fully to Christ's service. He writes, "I would that all men were even as I myself. But every man hath his own gift of God, one after this manner, and another after that" (1 Corinthians 7:7, KJV). Singleness, for Paul, was a gift that freed him to travel, preach, and endure persecution without the responsibilities of family. Yet, he recognizes that not all are called to this life, and marriage is a godly choice for those who lack the gift of celibacy.

This teaching counters Corinth's cultural extremes—both its indulgence in sexual sin and its occasional embrace of asceticism. Paul's own life, marked by passion for the law before his conversion and for Christ afterward, illustrates the power of redirecting one's desires toward God's purposes. He likely faced personal loss, as his wife died early, yet he found joy in serving Christ without the encumbrances of family. His words remind us that a family is a great blessing, but there are also weaknesses to marriage. A family takes time, energy, and resources. In times of persecution, a spouse or children could be used as leverage by enemies, making singleness a strategic advantage for ministry.

Paul's perspective challenges modern churches, where marriage is often seen as the default or superior state. Singleness, when embraced as a gift, allows undivided devotion to Christ. A fireproof church honors both marriage and singleness, recognizing that each is a calling from God, and encourages believers to serve faithfully in their God-given state.

## Marriage and Divorce: Staying Where God Called You

Paul addresses marriage and divorce with clarity, distinguishing between the Lord's command and his own Spirit-led opinion: "And unto the married I command, yet not I, but the Lord, Let not the wife depart from her husband: But and if she depart, let her remain unmarried, or be reconciled to her husband: and let not the husband put away his wife" (1 Corinthians 7:10–11, KJV). This echoes Jesus' teaching in Matthew 19:6, affirming marriage as a lifelong covenant. Some Corinthians, upon conversion, were divorcing unbelieving spouses, thinking their new faith required a "Christian" marriage. Paul corrects this: "But to the rest speak I, not the Lord: If any brother hath a wife that believeth not, and she be pleased to dwell with him, let him not put her away. And the woman which hath an husband that believeth not, and if he be pleased to dwell with her, let her not leave him" (1 Corinthians 7:12–13, KJV).

Paul explains that a believer's presence sanctifies the home: "For the unbelieving husband is sanctified by the wife, and the unbelieving wife is sanctified by the husband: else were your children unclean; but now are they holy" (1 Corinthians 7:14, KJV). This does not mean automatic salvation but that the believer brings God's grace into the household, offering opportunities for the unbeliever to encounter Christ. Under Roman law, children of a dissolved marriage could lose legal legitimacy, so staying married preserves the family's stability and witness. If an unbeliever insists on divorce, however, Paul advises, "But if the unbelieving depart, let him depart. A brother or a sister is not under bondage in such cases: but God hath called us to peace" (1 Corinthians 7:15, KJV). God desires peace, not strife, in the believer's life.

This teaching challenges the Corinthians' tendency to disrupt their marriages for spiritual reasons, harming their testimony. It also speaks to modern believers who face mixed marriages, encouraging them to live out their faith winsomely, trusting God to work through their presence. A fireproof church supports believers in mixed marriages, praying for their spouses' salvation while honoring God's call to peace.

## Contentment in Calling: Bloom Where You're Planted

Paul broadens his counsel to encompass all life circumstances: "But as God hath distributed to every man, as the Lord hath called every one, so let him walk. And so ordain I in all churches" (1 Corinthians 7:17, KJV). He illustrates with circumcision and slavery: "Is any man called being circumcised? Let him not become uncircumcised. Is any called in uncircumcision? Let him not be circumcised.

Circumcision is nothing, and uncircumcision is nothing, but the keeping of the commandments of God" (1 Corinthians 7:18–19, KJV). Similarly, "Art thou called being a servant? Care not for it: but if thou mayest be made free, use it rather. For he that is called in the Lord, being a servant, is the Lord's freeman: likewise also he that is called, being free, is Christ's servant" (1 Corinthians 7:21–22, KJV).

In Corinth's stratified society, where status was everything, these instructions were radical. Jews and Gentiles, slaves and free, were equal in Christ, and their external circumstances did not define their calling. Paul's principle—"bloom where you're planted"—urges believers to serve God faithfully in their current state. A slave, though bound to a human master, is free in Christ; a free person is Christ's servant. This perspective transforms how we view our circumstances, as Paul reminds them, "Ye are bought with a price; be not ye the servants of men" (1 Corinthians 7:23, KJV). Christ's blood, the ultimate price, frees us to serve Him alone.

This challenges modern believers who seek to change their circumstances—whether marital status, employment status, or social position—believing they would be happier if their conditions were different. Such restlessness reveals a failure to find true joy in God, who alone is the source of lasting contentment. A fireproof church encourages believers to rest in God's sufficient calling, trusting that His purpose for their lives—whether single or married, slave or free, employed or unemployed—is enough. By anchoring our joy in Christ rather than fleeting circumstances, we serve Him faithfully in every situation, building a church that stands resilient in a passing world.

# Joseph's Faith: Contentment in God's Plan

To illustrate the power of contentment in God's calling, consider the life of Joseph, whose story in Genesis 37–50 exemplifies unwavering faith in the face of crushing circumstances. Joseph's journey was marked by rejection, slavery, betrayal, and imprisonment, yet he remained faithful, unaware of the glorious plan God was unfolding. Sold into slavery by his own brothers, he was torn from his family and homeland, facing rejection that cut deep (Genesis 37:27–28). As a slave in Potiphar's house, he served faithfully, only to be betrayed by false accusations and cast into prison (Genesis 39:17–20). Even in prison, he endured years of confinement, forgotten by those he helped (Genesis 40:23). Through it all, Joseph had no inkling that God was preparing him to save nations from famine and reconcile his family (Genesis 45:7).

Joseph's faith shines as a model for the Corinthians and for us. He could have despaired, believing he would be happier if his conditions were different—if he were free, reunited with his family, or spared betrayal. Yet, he found his joy in God, serving faithfully wherever he was placed. In Potiphar's house, "the Lord was with Joseph, and he was a prosperous man" (Genesis 39:2, KJV). In prison, "the Lord was with him, and that which he did, the Lord made it to prosper" (Genesis 39:23, KJV). Joseph's contentment was not in his circumstances but in God's presence, trusting that God was working even when the plan was hidden.

For believers today, Joseph's example is magnified by the assurance of Romans 8:28: "And we know that all things work together for good to them that love God, to them who are called according to his purpose" (KJV). Unlike Joseph, who could not see the end of his story, we know that God is weaving all things—rejection, hardship, or delay—into a glorious tapestry that culminates in our eternal redemption (Romans 8:30). This gives us even greater reason to rest in God and serve where we are, whether in marriage, singleness, or any station of life. A fireproof church draws strength from this truth, trusting God's unseen plan and finding joy in Him alone.

## Living Lightly: The World Is Passing Away

Paul concludes with an eternal perspective: "But this I say, brethren, the time is short: it remaineth, that both they that have wives be as though they had none; And they that weep, as though they wept not; and they that rejoice, as though they rejoiced not; and they that buy, as though they possessed not; And they that use this world, as not abusing it: for the fashion of this world passeth away" (1 Corinthians 7:29–31, KJV). The "impending crisis" Paul mentions likely refers to persecution or societal upheaval, though its exact nature is unclear. His point is that this world is temporary, and believers must hold it lightly, prioritizing Christ's kingdom.

This call to live lightly resonates in our consumer-driven culture, where possessions, relationships, and achievements often define us. Paul urges, "Live as though you don't own anything, as though the day is coming—be ready to leave it all behind." The trumpet will sound, and we will be "caught up together with them in the clouds, to meet the Lord in the air" (1 Thessalonians 4:17, KJV), taking nothing but what we've sent ahead through service to Christ. A fireproof church lives with this eternal perspective, free from the entanglements of a passing world.

Paul adds, "I would have you without carefulness. He that is unmarried careth for the things that belong to the Lord, how he may please the Lord: But he that is married careth for the things that are of the world, how he may please his wife" (1 Corinthians 7:32–33, KJV). Singleness offers freedom for undivided devotion, but marriage is no less holy. Both are callings to serve God, and a fireproof church supports all members in their God-given roles, fostering contentment and purpose.

## Widows and Remarriage: Marrying in the Lord

Paul addresses widows: "The wife is bound by the law as long as her husband liveth; but if her husband be dead, she is at liberty to be married to whom she will; only in the Lord. Yet she is happier, in my judgment, if she so abide, after my judgment: and I think also that I have the Spirit of God" (1 Corinthians 7:39–40, KJV). A widow is free to remarry, but only to a believer, ensuring spiritual unity.

Paul, likely a widower himself, suggests that remaining single may bring greater happiness by avoiding the complexities of a new family, but he leaves room for personal choice.

This counsel reflects Paul's pastoral balance: affirming freedom while guiding believers toward what is most beneficial. A fireproof church supports widows and singles, encouraging them to marry "in the Lord" if they choose, while affirming the value of singleness for God's service.

## Conclusion: A Church Ready for Eternity

The Corinthian church, like ours, was called to be a fireproof church—content, faithful, and anchored in eternity. In a city driven by ambition and pleasure, Paul urged them to hold marriage, singleness, and all circumstances lightly, serving Christ above all. His words in 1 Corinthians 7 challenge us to find contentment in God's calling, to live as His purchased people, and to prepare for the day when this world passes away. As members of Christ's body, we are not our own but His, called to glorify Him in every aspect of life. Let us build a church that shines with eternal purpose, ready for the trumpet's call.

## Application: Building a Fireproof Church

A fireproof church lives contentedly, prioritizing Christ in every circumstance. Here are four ways to apply 1 Corinthians 7:

- **Honor Marriage and Singleness**: Value both as God-given callings. Support married couples in their mutual submission and singles in their devotion to Christ, recognizing each as a gift for His glory.

- **Stay Where God Called You**: Whether married, single, slave, or free, serve God faithfully in your current state. Bloom where you're planted, trusting God's purpose for your life.

- **Live in Peace with Unbelievers**: In mixed marriages, live out your faith winsomely, sanctifying your home through God's grace. Trust

Him to work through your witness, even if your spouse departs.

- **Hold the World Lightly**: Live as pilgrims, ready to leave everything behind when Christ returns. Focus on what you can send ahead through service, not what you can accumulate here.

## Prayer

*Father, we thank You for calling us to live for eternity, content in Your purpose. Help us to honor marriage and singleness, to stay where You've called us, and to hold this world lightly. Build us into a fireproof church that glorifies You. In Jesus' name,*

*Amen.*

# 9

## Called to Sacrifice: Love over Liberty

### A Church Built on Love

The Corinthian church, nestled in a city saturated with idolatry and pride, faced a critical test: could it prioritize love over personal freedom in a culture that exalted self-interest? In 1 Corinthians 8 and 9, Paul addresses a pressing question about eating food sacrificed to idols, revealing a deeper issue: the tension between knowledge and love, rights and responsibility. His teaching challenges the Corinthians to lay aside their liberties for the sake of weaker believers and the gospel's advance, a principle he illustrates through his own life of sacrifice. For a church to be fireproof, it must place love above knowledge, choosing to build up others rather than asserting personal rights, and live with an eternal perspective in a world of fleeting idols.

This chapter explores 1 Corinthians 8 and 9, where Paul tackles the Corinthians' question about idol-sacrificed food and uses his apostolic example to model sacrificial love. We will examine the cultural context of Corinth's idol-worshipping society, the dangers of knowledge without love, and the call to prioritize the spiritual growth of others. Drawing on Moses' choice to abandon his privileged position for the sake of God's people, we will see how trusting God's unseen plan enables us to sacrifice personal gain for His glory. Knowing the end of our story through Romans 8:28, we have even greater reason to lay aside our rights for Christ's sake. A fireproof church is one that loves sacrificially, guards the consciences of the weak, and advances the gospel above all.

*Now as touching things offered unto idols, we know that we all have knowledge. Knowledge puffeth up, but charity edifieth. And if any man think that he knoweth any thing, he knoweth nothing yet as he ought to know. But if any man love God, the same is known of him. As concerning therefore the eating of those things that are offered in sacrifice unto idols, we know that an idol is nothing in the world, and that there is none other God but one. For though there be that are called gods, whether in heaven or in earth, (as there be gods many, and lords many,)*

*But to us there is but one God, the Father, of whom are all things, and we in him; and one*

*Lord Jesus Christ, by whom are all things, and we by him. Howbeit there is not in every man that knowledge: for some with conscience of the idol unto this hour eat it as a thing offered unto an idol; and their conscience being weak is defiled. But meat commendeth us not to God: for neither, if we eat, are we the better; neither, if we eat not, are we the worse. But take heed lest by any means this liberty of yours become a stumbling block to them that are weak. For if any man see thee which hast knowledge sit at meat in the idol's temple, shall not the conscience of him which is weak be emboldened to eat those things which are offered to idols? And through thy knowledge shall the weak brother perish, for whom Christ died? But when ye sin so against the brethren, and wound their weak conscience, ye sin against Christ. Wherefore, if meat make my brother to offend, I will eat no flesh while the world standeth, lest I make my brother to offend. (I Corinthians 8, KJV)*

# The Corinthian Question: Food Sacrificed to Idols

Paul begins 1 Corinthians 8 with a response to another question from the Corinthians' letter: "Now as touching things offered unto idols, we know that we all have knowledge. Knowledge puffeth up, but charity edifieth" (1 Corinthians 8:1, KJV). The issue was food sacrificed to idols, a common practice in Corinth's pagan culture. As we noted in Chapter 1, Corinth was a city of temples, with the temple of Aphrodite and others on every corner. Animals were sacrificed daily, and the leftover meat, after priests took their share, was sold cheaply in the market or served at community feasts. For poorer Christians, this "idol meat" was an affordable option, but it sparked a heated debate in the church.

Some Corinthians, armed with theological knowledge, argued, "An idol is nothing in the world, and that there is none other God but one" (1 Corinthians 8:4, KJV). They were correct: idols were mere statues, powerless compared to the one true God. They felt free to eat this meat, knowing it had no spiritual significance. However, others—newer believers recently converted from idolatry—struggled. For them, eating such meat felt like participating in idol worship, violating their consciences. Paul warns, "But take heed lest by any means this liberty of yours become a stumblingblock to them that are weak" (1 Corinthians 8:9, KJV). If a weaker believer saw a knowledgeable Christian dining in an idol's temple, their conscience might be "emboldened" to eat, leading them back to idolatry (1 Corinthians 8:10, KJV).

This issue, though foreign to modern Western culture, mirrors contemporary debates over Christian liberty.

We may not face idol-sacrificed meat, but we encounter issues where personal freedoms—such as certain behaviors, media choices, or cultural practices —can harm others' faith. Paul's principle is clear: "Knowledge puffeth up, but charity edifieth" (1 Corinthians 8:1, KJV). Knowledge without love breeds pride, but love builds up the body. A fireproof church prioritizes love over rights, ensuring that its freedoms do not lead others to stumble.

## The Danger of Knowledge Without Love

Paul acknowledges the truth of the Corinthians' knowledge: "For though there be that are called gods, whether in heaven or in earth, (as there be gods many, and lords many,) But to us there is but one God, the Father, of whom are all things, and we in him; and one Lord Jesus Christ, by whom are all things, and we by him" (1 Corinthians 8:5–6, KJV). Yet, he cautions, "Howbeit there is not in every man that knowledge: for some with conscience of the idol unto this hour eat it as a thing offered unto an idol; and their conscience being weak is defiled" (1 Corinthians 8:7, KJV). For those steeped in idolatry from childhood, eating this meat carried spiritual weight, defiling their conscience and potentially drawing them back to pagan practices.

Paul's concern is not just the act of eating but its impact: "But when ye sin so against the brethren, and wound their weak conscience, ye sin against Christ" (1 Corinthians 8:12, KJV). By exercising their liberty carelessly, the knowledgeable Corinthians risked destroying a weaker believer "for whom Christ died" (1 Corinthians 8:11, KJV). This is a grave sin, as it undermines Christ's sacrifice. Paul's radical commitment is striking: "Wherefore, if meat make my brother to offend, I will eat no flesh while the world standeth, lest I make my brother to offend" (1 Corinthians 8:13, KJV). He would rather abandon meat entirely than harm a brother's faith.

This principle challenges our modern obsession with personal rights. In Corinth, as in our world, believers often prioritize "what's best for me," saying, "I have the right to do this; it's not a sin." Yet, Paul warns that our will—our autonomy, independence, or liberty—can become an idol as dangerous as any statue in a Corinthian temple. A fireproof church recognizes that love, not knowledge, is the measure of maturity, choosing to build up others over asserting personal freedoms.

## Spiritual Powers Behind Idols

Paul adds a sobering note: while idols are nothing, they are not powerless. He acknowledges, "As concerning therefore the eating of those things that are offered in sacrifice unto idols, we know that an idol is nothing in the world" (1 Corinthians 8:4, KJV), but he also notes, "For though there be that are called gods, whether in heaven or on earth, (as there be many gods, and many lords)" (1 Corinthians 8:5, KJV). Behind these false gods are spiritual forces—demonic powers that deceive and draw people away from God. Participating in idol-related practices, even with a clear conscience, risks sending a mixed message to weaker believers and unbelievers alike, who might think, "Christians can worship idols too."

This warning applies today. While we may not face temple sacrifices, cultural practices—whether certain symbols, entertainment, or ideologies—can carry spiritual weight. Displaying a statue or engaging in activities tied to false beliefs may seem harmless, but Paul cautions that these can invite spiritual danger. A fireproof church is vigilant, recognizing the reality of spiritual forces and guarding its testimony by avoiding practices that confuse or compromise its witness.

## Paul's Example: Sacrificing Apostolic Rights

In 1 Corinthians 9, Paul illustrates this principle through his own life: "Am I not an apostle? Am I not free? Have I not seen Jesus Christ our Lord? Are not ye my work in the Lord?" (1 Corinthians 9:1, KJV). He defends his apostleship, noting that the Corinthian church itself is evidence of his calling: "If I be not an apostle unto others, yet doubtless I am to you: for the seal of mine apostleship are ye in the Lord" (1 Corinthians 9:2, KJV). As an apostle, Paul had greater rights than most, including financial support and the companionship of a believing wife: "Have we not power to eat and to drink? Have we not power to lead about a sister, a wife, as well as other apostles, and as the brethren of the Lord, and Cephas?" (1 Corinthians 9:4–5, KJV).

Paul uses biblical and common-sense examples to affirm these rights: "Who goeth a warfare any time at his own charges? Who planteth a vineyard, and eateth not of the fruit thereof? Or who feedeth a flock, and eateth not of the milk of the flock? … For it is written in the law of Moses, Thou shalt not muzzle the mouth of the ox that treadeth out the corn. Doth God take care for oxen?" (1 Corinthians 9:7–9, KJV). Yet, he declares, "Nevertheless we have not used this right; but suffer all things, lest we should hinder the gospel of Christ" (1 Corinthians 9:12, KJV). In Corinth, Paul worked as a tentmaker with Aquila and Priscilla (Acts 18:3), refusing support to avoid burdening the church or hindering the gospel.

Paul's sacrifice was not about personal gain but about the gospel's advance: "For though I preach the gospel, I have nothing to glory of: for necessity is laid upon me; yea, woe is unto me, if I preach not the gospel!" (1 Corinthians 9:16, KJV). His reward was offering the gospel freely: "What is my reward then? Verily that, when I preach the gospel, I may make the gospel of Christ without charge, that I abuse not my power in the gospel" (1 Corinthians 9:18, KJV). By becoming "all things to all men" (1 Corinthians 9:22, KJV), Paul tailored his ministry to reach Jews, Gentiles, and the weak, always within God's law, to save some. A fireproof church follows Paul's example, sacrificing personal rights to prioritize the gospel and the spiritual growth of others.

## Moses' Faith: Choosing God's People Over Privilege

Paul's willingness to forgo his apostolic rights mirrors the faith of Moses, whose story in Exodus and Hebrews 11 exemplifies the choice to sacrifice privilege for the sake of God's people. Raised as "the son of Pharaoh's daughter" (Hebrews 11:24, KJV), Moses enjoyed wealth, power, and influence in Egypt's royal court. He could have justified remaining in this position, using his authority to ease the Hebrews' suffering under slavery. Such a choice would have been comfortable, even noble, in the eyes of the world. Yet, Moses chose a harder path: "By faith Moses, when he was come to years, refused to be called the son of Pharaoh's daughter; Choosing rather to suffer an affliction with the people of God, than to enjoy the pleasures of sin for a season;

Esteeming the reproach of Christ greater riches than the treasures in Egypt: for he had respect unto the recompense of the reward" (Hebrews 11:24–26, KJV).

Moses became an outcast and a wanderer, fleeing Egypt after killing an Egyptian oppressor (Exodus 2:15), and later leading Israel through the wilderness for forty years. He had no assurance of immediate success, yet he trusted God's unseen plan, prioritizing the liberation of God's people over personal comfort. His faith sustained him through rejection, uncertainty, and hardship, as he looked to an eternal reward. For believers today, Moses' example is magnified by Romans 8:28: "And we know that all things work together for good to them that love God, to them who are the called according to his purpose" (KJV). Unlike Moses, who acted without seeing the full scope of God's plan, we know that our sacrifices for others and the gospel contribute to God's redemptive purpose. This gives us even greater reason to lay aside our rights, trusting that God is working for our good and His glory. A fireproof church draws strength from Moses' faith, choosing love for others over personal privilege, as Paul did in Corinth.

## Running to Win: The Imperishable Crown

Paul concludes 1 Corinthians 9 with an athletic metaphor, fitting for Corinth, home of the Isthmian

Games: "Know ye not that they which run in a race run all, but one receiveth the prize? So run, that ye may obtain. And every man that striveth for the mastery is temperate in all things. Now they do it to obtain a corruptible crown; but we an imperishable" (1 Corinthians 9:24–25, KJV). Athletes exercise self-control for a perishable prize, but believers discipline themselves for an eternal reward—the "imperishable crown" of souls won to Christ. Paul declares, "I therefore so run, not as uncertainly; so fight I, not as one that beateth the air: But I keep under my body, and bring it into subjection: lest that by any means, when I have preached to others, I myself should be a castaway" (1 Corinthians 9:26–27, KJV).

This call to self-discipline challenges the Corinthians' pride in their knowledge and rights. By submitting his desires to Christ, Paul ensured his life advanced the gospel, not hindered it. A fireproof church runs with purpose, sacrificing personal desires to win others to Christ, valuing the eternal reward over temporary freedoms.

## Conclusion: A Church of Sacrificial Love

The Corinthian church, like ours, was called to be a fireproof church—loving, sacrificial, and focused on eternity. In a city of idols and pride, Paul urged them to lay aside their liberties for the sake of weaker believers and the gospel's advance. Moses' choice to abandon Egypt's treasures for God's people shows the power of trusting God's unseen plan. Knowing that "all things work together for good" (Romans 8:28, KJV), we have every reason to sacrifice our rights for Christ's sake. As members of Christ's body, we are called to build up one another, not to assert our rights. Let us build a church that runs to win, glorifying Christ in a world of perishable idols.

## Application: Building a Fireproof Church

A fireproof church prioritizes love over liberty, building up others for the gospel's sake. Here are four ways to apply 1 Corinthians 8 and 9:

- **Choose Love Over Knowledge**: Recognize that knowledge without love puffs up. Lay aside freedoms that might cause weaker believers to stumble, prioritizing their spiritual growth.

- **Guard Against Spiritual Dangers**: Avoid practices that could confuse your testimony or invite spiritual harm, acknowledging the reality of spiritual forces behind false beliefs.

**Sacrifice for the Gospel: Like Paul, forgo personal rights—whether financial, social, or otherwise—to advance the gospel, becoming all things to all people to save some.**

- **Run for the Imperishable Crown**: Like Joseph, rest in God's plan, trusting Romans 8:28. Discipline yourself to serve faithfully where you are, valuing eternal rewards over temporary gains.

## Prayer

*Father, we thank You for calling us to love sacrificially, laying aside our liberties for others. Like Paul and Joseph, help us to trust Your plan and find joy in You alone. Build us into a fireproof church that advances Your gospel. In Jesus' name,*

*Amen.*

# 10

## Called to Communion: One Bread and One Life

### A Church United in Christ

The Corinthian church, planted in a city of division and idolatry, faced a critical challenge: could it maintain its unity as God's people in a culture that celebrated self-interest and false gods? In 1 Corinthians 10, Paul warns the Corinthians by pointing to Israel's failures in the wilderness, where they forgot their unique identity as God's redeemed people, falling into discontent and idolatry. He calls the church to embrace its identity in Christ, exemplified in the Lord's Supper, where believers share "one bread and one life" through the body and blood of the Savior. For a church to be fireproof, it must guard its unity, reject idolatry, and live committed to Christ for the sake of the body.

This chapter explores 1 Corinthians 10, where Paul uses Israel's history to caution against discontent and idolatry, urging the Corinthians to live out their unity in Christ. We will examine the cultural pressures of Corinth's idol-worshipping society, the significance of the Lord's Supper as a symbol of fellowship, and the call to prioritize the body's unity over personal desires. Drawing on Moses' choice to sacrifice privilege for God's people, we will see how trusting God's plan enables us to live for others.

Knowing that "all things work together for good" (Romans 8:28, KJV), we have every reason to remain steadfast in our commitment to Christ and His church. A fireproof church is one that lives as one body, united in the strength of Christ's bread and the life of His blood.

*Am I not an apostle? Am I not free? Have I not seen Jesus Christ our Lord? Are not ye my work in the Lord? If I be not an apostle unto others, yet doubtless I am to you: for the seal of mine apostleship are ye in the Lord.*

*Mine answer to them that do examine me is this,*

*Have we not power to eat and to drink?*

*Have we not power to lead about a sister, a wife, as well as other apostles, and as the brethren of the Lord, and Cephas?*

*Or I only and Barnabas, have not we power to forbear working?*

*Who goeth a warfare any time at his own charges? Who planteth a vineyard, and eateth not of the fruit thereof? Or who feedeth a flock, and eateth not of the milk of the flock? Say I these things as a man? Or saith not the law the same also? For it is written in the law of Moses, thou shalt not muzzle the mouth of the ox that treadeth out the corn. Doth God take care for oxen? Or saith he it altogether for our sakes? For our sakes, no doubt, this is written: that he that ploweth should plow in hope; and that he that thresheth in hope should be partaker of his hope. If we have sown unto you spiritual things, is it a great thing if we shall reap your carnal things? If others be partakers of this power over you, are not we rather? Nevertheless, we have not used this power; but suffer all things, lest we should hinder the gospel of Christ. Do ye not know that they which minister about holy things live of the things of the temple? And they which wait at the altar are partakers with the altar? Even so hath the Lord ordained that they which preach the gospel should live of the gospel. But I have used none of these things: neither have I written these things, that it should be so done unto me: for it were better for me to die, than that any man should make my glorying void. For though I preach the gospel, I have nothing to glory of: for necessity is laid upon me; yea, woe is unto me, if I preach not the gospel! For if I do this thing willingly, I have a reward: but if against my will, a dispensation of the gospel is committed unto me. What is my reward then?*

*Verily, that when I preach the gospel, I may make the gospel of Christ without charge, that I abuse not my power in the gospel. For though I be free from all men, yet have I made myself a servant unto all, that I might gain the more. And unto the Jews I became as a Jew, that I might gain the Jews; to them that are under the law, as under the law, that I might gain them that are under the law; to them that are without law, as without law, (being not without law to God, but under the law to Christ,) that I might gain them that are without law. To the weak became I as weak, that I might gain the weak: I am made all things to all men, that I might by all means save some. And this I do for the gospel's sake, that I might be partaker thereof with you. Know ye not that they which run in a race run all, but one receiveth the prize? So run, that ye may obtain. And every man that striveth for the mastery is temperate in all things. Now they do it to obtain a corruptible crown; but we an incorruptible. I therefore so run, not as uncertainly; so fight I, not as one that beateth the air: But I keep under my body, and bring it into subjection: lest that by any means, when I have preached to others, I myself should be a castaway. (1 Corinthians 10, KJV)*

## Israel's Failure: Forgetting Their Identity

Paul opens 1 Corinthians 10 with a sobering lesson from Israel's history: "Moreover, brethren, I would not that ye should be ignorant, how that all our fathers were under the cloud, and all passed through the sea; And were all baptized unto Moses in the cloud and in the sea; And did all eat the same spiritual meat; And did all drink the same spiritual drink: for they drank of that spiritual Rock that followed them: and that Rock was Christ" (1 Corinthians 10:1–4, KJV). The Israelites, redeemed through the Exodus and protected in the wilderness, shared a common identity as God's chosen people. The cloud and sea symbolized their deliverance, the manna and water their sustenance, all pointing to Christ, the spiritual Rock.

Yet, despite these blessings, "with many of them God was not well pleased: for they were overthrown in the wilderness" (1 Corinthians 10:5, KJV). Why? They forgot their unique identity, growing discontent and turning to idolatry: "Neither be ye idolaters, as were some of them; as it is written, The people sat down to eat and drink, and rose up to play" (1 Corinthians

10:7, KJV). Referencing the golden calf incident (Exodus 32:6), Paul warns that Israel's craving for the pleasures of Egypt led them to worship false gods, resulting in judgment. Their discontent also fueled immorality and grumbling: "Neither let us commit fornication, as some of them committed, and fell in one day three and twenty thousand. Neither let us tempt Christ, as some of them also tempted, and were destroyed of serpents. Neither murmur ye, as some of them also murmured, and were destroyed of the destroyer" (1 Corinthians 10:8–10, KJV).

Corinth's culture, as explored in Chapter 1, mirrored Egypt's idolatry. Temples to Aphrodite and other gods filled the city, and the Corinthians, like Israel, were tempted to blend their faith with pagan practices. Paul's warning is clear: "Now all these things happened unto them for ensamples: and they are written for our admonition, upon whom the ends of the world are come" (1 Corinthians 10:11, KJV). A fireproof church remembers its identity as God's redeemed people, resisting the pull of discontent and idolatry that threatens its unity.

## The Lord's Supper: One Bread and One Life

Paul shifts to the heart of Christian identity: "The cup of blessing which we bless, is it not the communion of the blood of Christ? The bread which we break, is it not the communion of the body of Christ?" (1 Corinthians 10:16, KJV). The Greek text underscores this unity: τὸ ποτήριον τῆς εὐλογίας ὃ εὐλογοῦμεν, οὐχὶκοινωνία ἐστιν τοῦ αἵματος τοῦ χριστοῦ; τὸν ἄρτον ὃν κλῶμεν, οὐχὶ κοινωνία τοῦ σώματος τοῦχριστοῦ ἐστιν—the cup and bread are a *koinonia*, a fellowship or participation in Christ's blood and body. The bread represents Christ's body, our source of strength; the cup, His blood, the life that redeems us, for "the life of the flesh is in the blood" (Leviticus 17:11, KJV). By partaking in the Lord's Supper, believers proclaim their unity with Christ and one another: "For we being many are one bread, and one body: for we are all partakers of that one bread" (1 Corinthians 10:17, KJV).

In Corinth, where dining at idol temples was common, Paul contrasts the Lord's Supper with pagan feasts: "Ye cannot drink the cup of the Lord, and the cup of devils: ye cannot be partakers of the Lord's table, and of the table of devils" (1 Corinthians 10:21, KJV). Participating in idol feasts, even with a clear conscience (as discussed in Chapter 6), risks compromising the church's testimony and unity. The Lord's Supper binds believers to Christ and each other, demanding exclusive allegiance. A fireproof church guards this sacred fellowship, rejecting any practice that dilutes its commitment to Christ.

# Fleeing Idolatry: Commitment to the Body

Paul urges, "Wherefore, my dearly beloved, flee from idolatry" (1 Corinthians 10:14, KJV). This call echoes his concern in 1 Corinthians 8 about food sacrificed to idols, which could lead weaker believers to stumble. Here, he broadens the warning: idolatry is not just physical statues but anything that takes precedence over Christ—whether personal desires, cultural practices, or worldly pleasures. The Corinthians, like Israel, risked dividing their loyalty, undermining the unity symbolized in the Lord's Supper.

Paul's practical guidance follows: "All things are lawful for me, but all things are not expedient: all things are lawful for me, but all things edify not. Let no man seek his own, but every man another's wealth" (1 Corinthians 10:23–24, KJV). Christian liberty, while real, must serve the body's good. Eating idol meat in a temple, though permissible for some, could confuse unbelievers or harm weaker Christians, as "Uncle Joe" might say, "I thought Christians didn't do this anymore!" Our commitment to Christ, expressed in the Lord's Supper, extends to our brothers and sisters, requiring us to prioritize their spiritual growth over our freedoms.

This principle challenges modern believers. We may not dine in idol temples, but we face idols of ambition, entertainment, or self-assertion that threaten our unity.

A fireproof church flees these idols, choosing to build up the body rather than seeking personal gain, ensuring that its witness remains clear.

## Living for Others: The Gospel's Advance

Paul concludes with a call to glorify God in all things: "Whether therefore ye eat, or drink, or whatsoever ye do, do all to the glory of God. Give none offence, neither to the Jews, nor to the Gentiles, nor to the church of God: Even as I please all men in all things, not seeking mine own profit, but the profit of many, that they may be saved" (1 Corinthians 10:31–33, KJV). Like his example in 1 Corinthians 9, where he forwent apostolic rights, Paul urges the Corinthians to live for others' salvation, not their own gain. This aligns with the Lord's Supper, where sharing one bread and one cup commits us to the body's welfare.

In Corinth's competitive culture, this was radical. Today, we face similar pressures to prioritize self—career, status, or personal freedom. Yet, Paul calls us to live as one body, united in Christ's strength and life, ensuring our actions edify others and advance the gospel. A fireproof church lives for Christ's glory, sacrificing personal desires to strengthen the body and reach the lost.

# Conclusion: A Church of One Bread and One Life

The Corinthian church, like ours, was called to be a fireproof church—united, holy, and devoted to Christ. In a city of idols, Paul warned against Israel's failures, urging the Corinthians to embrace their identity in the Lord's Supper, where one bread and one cup signify strength and life in Christ. Moses' choice to suffer with God's people over Egypt's treasures inspires us to prioritize the body's unity. Knowing that "all things work together for good" (Romans 8:28, KJV), we have every reason to live for Christ and His church. Let us build a fireproof church that glorifies God, united as one body in a world of fleeting idols.

# Application: Building a Fireproof Church

A fireproof church is united in Christ, rejecting idolatry for the sake of the body. Here are four ways to apply 1 Corinthians 10:

- **Remember Your Identity**: Like Israel, recall your redemption in Christ, symbolized in the Lord's Supper. Let this unity guide your actions, guarding against discontent and idolatry.

- **Guard the Lord's Supper**: Approach the Lord's table with reverence, recognizing it as communion, or sharing, in Christ's body and blood. Reject practices that compromise this fellowship.

- **Sacrifice for Unity:** Like Moses, forgo personal privileges to build up the body. Prioritize others' spiritual growth over your freedoms, trusting Romans 8:28.

- **Live for God's Glory**: In all things—eating, drinking, or living—seek to glorify God and edify others, advancing the gospel without causing offense.

# Prayer

*Father, we thank You for uniting us as one body through Christ's body and blood. Help us to flee idolatry, live for others, and glorify You. Build us into a fireproof church, strong in Your strength and alive in Your life. In Jesus' name,*

*Amen.*

# 11

## Worshipping as a Fireproof Church

### Worship That Strengthens the Fireproof Church

In the heart of Corinth, where pride and division burned like wildfires, the church's worship became a battleground. Some flaunted cultural norms, disregarding God's order; others turned the Lord's Supper into a selfish feast, shaming the poor. These were fires of disunity and irreverence, threatening to consume the church's witness. Yet Paul, in 1 Corinthians 11, calls the Corinthians—and us—to worship as a fireproof church, united in Christ, reverent in His presence, and inclusive of all. Worship is not a stage for personal agendas but a sacred act that reflects the foundation of Christ (Chapter 4) and the unity of "one bread, one body" (Chapter 10). This chapter explores how a fireproof church worships with order, respect, and hope, enduring the fires of division and shining God's glory in a fractured world.

*Be ye followers of me, even as I also am of Christ.*

*Now I praise you, brethren, that ye remember me in all things, and keep the ordinances, as I delivered them to you.*

*But I would have you know that the head of every man is Christ; and the head of the woman is the man; and the head of Christ is God. Every man praying or prophesying, having his head covered, dishonoureth his head. But every woman that prayeth or prophesieth with her head uncovered dishonoureth her head: for that is even all one as if she were shaven.*

*For if the woman be not covered, let her also be shorn: but if it be a shame for a woman to be shorn or shaven, let her be covered. For a man indeed ought not to cover his head, forasmuch as he is the image and glory of God: but the woman is the glory of the man.*

*For the man is not of the woman: but the woman of the man. Neither was the man created for the woman; but the woman for the man. For this cause ought the woman to have power on her head because of the angels.*

*Nevertheless neither is the man without the woman, neither the woman without the man, in the Lord. For as the woman is of the man, even so is the man also by the woman; but all things of God. Judge in yourselves: is it comely that a woman pray unto God uncovered? Doth not even nature itself teach you that if a man have long hair, it is a shame unto him? But if a woman have long hair, it is a glory to her: for her hair is given her for a covering.*

*But if any man seem to be contentious, we have no such custom, neither the churches of God.*

*Now in this that I declare unto you I praise you not that ye come together not for the better, but for the worse. For first of all, when ye come together in the church, I hear that there be divisions among you; and I partly believe it. For there must be also heresies among you, that they which are approved may be made manifest among you.*

*When ye come together therefore into one place, this is not to eat the Lord's supper. For in eating every one taketh before other his own supper: and one is hungry, and another is drunken. What? Have ye not houses to eat and to drink in? Or despise ye the church of God, and shame them that have not? What shall I say to you? Shall I praise you in this? I praise you not.*

*For I have received of the Lord that which also I delivered unto you, that the Lord Jesus the same night in which he was betrayed took bread: And when he had given thanks, he brake it, and said, Take, eat: this is my body, which is broken for you: this do in remembrance of me. After the same manner also he took the cup, when he had supped, saying, this cup is the new testament in my blood: this do ye, as oft as ye drink it, in remembrance of me. For as often as ye eat this bread, and drink this cup, ye do shew the Lord's death till he come.*

*Wherefore whosoever shall eat this bread, and drink this cup of the Lord, unworthily, shall be guilty of the body and blood of the Lord.*

*But let a man examine himself, and so let him eat of that bread, and drink of that cup. For he that eateth and drinketh unworthily, eateth and drinketh damnation to himself, not discerning the Lord's body. For this cause many are weak and sickly among you, and many sleep. For if we would judge ourselves, we should not be judged. But when we are judged, we are chastened of the Lord, that we should not be condemned with the world.*

*Wherefore, my brethren, when ye come together to eat, tarry one for another.*

*And if any man hunger, let him eat at home;*
*that ye come not together unto condemnation.*
*And the rest will I set in order when I come. (I*
*Corinthians 11, KJV)*

# The Corinthian Crisis: Disunity in Worship

Paul addresses two practices in 1 Corinthians 11 that reveal the Corinthians' struggle with unity: head coverings in worship (vv. 2–16) and abuses at the Lord's Supper (vv. 17–34). Both reflect deeper issues of selfishness, cultural compromise, and disregard for the body of Christ, threatening the church's fireproof foundation.

# Order in Worship: Head Coverings and Unity

In Corinth, a city steeped in social hierarchies and cultural display (Chapter 1), worship practices became a flashpoint for division. Paul writes, "But I would have you know, that the head of every man is Christ; and the head of the woman is the man; and the head of Christ is God" (1 Corinthians 11:3, KJV). He addresses head coverings, a cultural symbol in first-century Corinth where women worshipping uncovered or men covering their

> *For a deeper discussion of this subject, see Appendix 3*

heads could signal rebellion, immodesty, or confusion, undermining the church's witness in a society sensitive to such practices.

These actions risked fueling the fires of disunity, threatening the church's fireproof foundation (Chapter 4). Paul's instruction calls for order in worship, rooted in respect for God's design and submission to one another, to ensure the church glorifies Christ as one body.

There are generally three approaches to this passage, each emphasizing respect and submission as vital for unity:

1. **Cultural Interpretation**: Scholars like Gordon Fee argue that head coverings were a local custom tied to modesty and propriety in Corinth's Greco-Roman context. In a city where "to act like a Corinthian" meant debauchery (Chapter 1), uncovered women risked being mistaken for prostitutes or signaling defiance, disrupting the church's unified witness. Fee notes, "The issue is one of cultural propriety... Paul wants the Corinthians to avoid actions that would bring shame or disrepute to the gospel" (The First Epistle to the Corinthians, NICNT, 1987, 506–7). By adhering to cultural norms in worship, the church showed respect for its community and maintained unity in its testimony.

2. **Creational Interpretation**: Others, like Thomas Schreiner, see Paul grounding head coverings in the creation order (1 Corinthians 11:7–9), reflecting God's design for gender roles in worship. Schreiner writes, "Paul appeals to creation to show that men and women are interdependent, yet distinct, in their roles, which promotes harmony in the church" (1 Corinthians, Tyndale NT Commentaries, 2018, 226). This view emphasizes submission to God's authority as revealed in creation, fostering unity by aligning worship with His divine order.

3. **Principial Interpretation**: A third view, held by scholars like Craig Keener, focuses on timeless principles of mutual respect and deference in worship, regardless of specific practices. Keener explains, "Paul's concern is that worship reflect the glory of God rather than self-promotion or cultural confusion" (1–2 Corinthians, NCBC, 2005, 92). By prioritizing deference to others—whether through head coverings or other acts of humility—the church avoids division and glorifies Christ.

While I may find myself drawn to one of these perspectives—perhaps the principial view for its focus on timeless principles applicable to our diverse modern contexts—all three approaches are rooted in the biblical call to respect and submission, which are essential for a fireproof church. The cultural interpretation emphasizes respect for the community's norms, ensuring the church's witness remains untainted by scandal, as Paul urges: "Give none offence, neither to the Jews, nor to the Gentiles, nor to the church of God" (1 Corinthians 10:32, KJV). The creational interpretation highlights submission to God's created order, fostering harmony as believers honor their roles under Christ's headship: "The head of every man is Christ" (1 Corinthians 11:3, KJV). The principial interpretation underscores mutual respect and deference, reflecting the humility of Christ, who "made himself of no reputation, and took upon him the form of a servant" (Philippians 2:7, KJV). Together, these views teach that worship must prioritize God's glory and the church's unity over personal agendas. When believers practice respect—whether for cultural expectations, God's design, or one another—and submit to Christ's authority, they extinguish the fires of division, building a church that stands firm in worship.

## The Lord's Supper and Unity (1 Corinthians 11:17–34)

Paul's tone grows stern as he confronts the Corinthians' abuses at the Lord's Supper: "When ye come together, it is not to eat the Lord's supper. For in eating every one taketh before other his own supper: and one is hungry, and another is drunken" (1 Corinthians 11:20–21, KJV). In Corinth, a city divided by wealth and status (Chapter 1), the Lord's Supper—

intended to proclaim Christ's unifying sacrifice and the church's hope in His return—became a stage for selfishness, fracturing the body of Christ. These abuses were fires of division, threatening the church's fireproof foundation laid in Christ (Chapter 4). To grasp the gravity of this crisis, we must examine the cultural context of Corinth's social hierarchy, the early church's practice of the Lord's Supper within the communal Love Feast, and the profound transformation Christ brought to this sacred rite, which calls us to worship as one body.

## Corinthian Social Practices and the Church's Divide

Corinth, a thriving trade hub on the isthmus between the Corinthian Gulf and the Aegean Sea, was a city of stark social contrasts (Chapter 1). Its economy, fueled by commerce and the Isthmian Games, created a hierarchy where wealthy elites—Roman citizens, merchants, and landowners—enjoyed leisure and control over their schedules, while slaves and laborers, who formed a significant portion of the population, toiled under rigid constraints (Bradley, Slavery and Society at Rome, 1994, 57–60; Engels, Roman Corinth, 1990, 89–92). Slaves had no weekends or days off; their workdays, often in households, workshops, or ports, extended late into the evening, leaving them little time for communal gatherings (Frier, A Natural History of Rome, 2000,

112). Wealthier Christians, free to arrive early for church meetings, brought lavish foods and wines, reflecting the opulent banquets of Corinth's elite, where status was flaunted through abundance (Garland, 1 Corinthians, BECNT, 2003, 541). In contrast, slaves and the poor arrived late, weary from labor, often finding themselves excluded from the meal.

The Corinthian church mirrored this diversity, with members like Gaius, a wealthy host (Romans 16:23), and slaves or freedmen who lacked social standing (1 Corinthians 7:21–22). Early Christian gatherings typically occurred in homes, with dining spaces like the triclinium (a formal dining room for a few) reserved for prominent guests and larger courtyards or atria for others (Osiek & Balch, Families in the New Testament World, 1997, 24–27). Wealthier members dined early in the triclinium, consuming their private meals, while late-arriving poor members found little food, if any, in the courtyard (Thiselton, The First Epistle to the Corinthians, NIGTC, 2000, 880). This practice echoed Corinth's competitive culture, where social rank dictated access to resources, but it betrayed the gospel's call to unity: "There is neither Jew nor Greek, there is neither bond nor free... for ye are all one in Christ Jesus" (Galatians 3:28, KJV). By prioritizing status over fellowship, the Corinthians turned worship into a fire of division, weakening the church's witness.

# The Lord's Supper as a Love Feast

In the early church, the Lord's Supper was not a standalone ritual but the culminating act of a communal meal known as the Love Feast (*Agapé*), rooted in the Jewish Passover and Jesus' Last Supper (Fee, The First Epistle to the Corinthians, NICNT, 2014, 589). Described as "feasts of charity" in Jude 12 (KJV), the Love Feast was a shared meal where believers brought food to fellowship, worship, and celebrate Christ's sacrifice through bread and wine (Lampe, From Paul to Valentinus, 2003, 36–39). Held weekly on the Lord's Day (Sunday), it embodied *koinonia*—fellowship as one body—and anticipated the eschatological wedding supper of the Lamb (Revelation 19:7–9). Gordon Fee notes, "The Lord's Supper was a regularly repeated meal in 'honor of the Lord,' eaten in the context of a fellowship meal, reflecting the unity of God's new people" (Fee, 589). This holy banquet united rich and poor, slave and free, in a foretaste of God's kingdom, where all will feast equally.

Yet in Corinth, the Love Feast became a mockery of its purpose. Wealthier members, arriving early, consumed their own lavish meals, some even to drunkenness (1 Corinthians 11:21), while late-arriving slaves and poor members—delayed by work—found themselves hungry and humiliated. David Garland writes, "The Lord's Supper was meant to be a visible sermon of Christ's sacrifice and the church's unity, but the Corinthians turned it into a display of social privilege, despising the church of God" (1 Corinthians, 543). This selfishness reflected Corinth's banquet culture, where elites dined extravagantly while excluding the lower classes (Engels, 94–95). By failing to share, the wealthy shamed "them that have not" (1 Corinthians 11:22, KJV), fracturing the unity meant to shine through the Love Feast.

## Christ's Transformation of the Passover

When Jesus instituted the Lord's Supper, He transformed the Passover into a new celebration, not by adding elements but by removing those fulfilled in His sacrifice, revealing its power to unite and give hope. The Passover included a lamb, symbolizing deliverance from Egypt, and bitter herbs, representing the suffering of slavery. Jesus, our Passover Lamb (1 Corinthians 5:7), removed the lamb from the meal, for He was slain once for all (Hebrews 10:10). He omitted the bitter herbs, having taken the bitterness of sin and death upon Himself (Isaiah 53:4–5). He retained the unleavened bread, symbolizing His broken body, which gives us strength, and the cup of blessing, representing His shed blood, which grants us life and joy in a new relationship with God (Leviticus 17:11; John 6:53–56). As Paul writes, "This is my body, which is broken for you... This cup is the new testament in my blood" (1 Corinthians 11:24–25, KJV). This streamlined rite focuses on Christ's finished work, uniting believers as one body and pointing to the hope of His return.

## Paul's Gospel Correction

Paul's response restores the Lord's Supper's true meaning: "For I have received of the Lord that which also I delivered unto you, That the Lord Jesus the same night in which he was betrayed took bread..." (1 Corinthians 11:23–25, KJV). He recounts Jesus' institution, emphasizing its dual focus: looking back to Christ's sacrifice—"do this in remembrance of me" (11:24)—and forward to His return— "ye do shew the Lord's death till he come"(11:26). The Supper proclaims Christ's death, which unites all believers as "one bread, one body" (1 Corinthians 10:17, Chapter 10), and anticipates the future banquet when all will feast equally in His kingdom (Revelation 19:9). Eating "in an unworthy manner" (11:27) by excluding others is a sin against Christ's body—both His sacrifice and the church—inviting judgment, as seen in the sickness and death of some Corinthians (11:30).

Paul urges self-examination: "Let a man examine himself, and so let him eat of that bread, and drink of that cup" (1 Corinthians 11:28, KJV). This calls for introspection and discernment of the body—Christ's sacrifice and the church's unity. Anthony Thiselton notes, "To eat without discerning the body means failing to recognize the church as the unified body of Christ, purchased by His blood" (The First Epistle to the Corinthians, NIGTC, 2000, 891). The Love Feast, meant to embody *koinonia*, became a fire of division when the wealthy shamed the poor. Paul's solution is practical: "When ye come together to eat, tarry one for another" (11:33, KJV). Waiting for all members—rich and poor, slave and free—ensures the Supper reflects the gospel's equality and the hope of Christ's return.

## Fireproof Worship Through Unity

The Corinthians' abuse of the Lord's Supper reflects the fires of selfishness and division that threaten any church. By prioritizing status over love, they despised the church of God (11:22), weakening the fireproof foundation of Christ (Chapter 4). The Lord's Supper, transformed by Christ to focus on His body and blood, unites believers in His sacrifice and hope. A fireproof church worships with reverence, ensuring the Love Feast includes all, proclaiming Christ's death and anticipating His return, extinguishing the fires of social division with the strength of His broken body and the life of His shed blood.

# Conclusion: A Worshipping Church That Endures

A fireproof church worships as one body, rooted in the foundation of Christ (Chapter 4) and united in His body and blood (Chapter 10). In Corinth, disunity and irreverence threatened worship, but Paul called them to order, respect,

and reverence. The Lord's Supper, a symbol of Christ's sacrifice and our future hope, binds us as one, proclaiming His death until He comes. Let us worship with hearts submitted to God, inclusive of all, and fixed on the hope of His return. As we reject the fires of division and selfishness, we become a fireproof church, shining Christ's light in a divided world.

# Application: Building a Fireproof Church Through Worship

A fireproof church worships in a way that unites its members and glorifies God. Here are four ways to apply 1 Corinthians 11:

- **Worship with Reverence**: Approach God's presence with awe, whether in singing, prayer, or the Lord's Supper. Let Hebrews 12:28 guide you: "Let us have grace, whereby we may serve God acceptably with reverence and godly fear" (KJV).

Avoid casual or self-focused practices that diminish worship's purpose.

- **Honor the Body**: Ensure worship includes all members, rich and poor, young and old. Like the Lord's Supper, make no one feel less than another, reflecting the unity of "one bread, one body" (1 Corinthians 10:17).

- **Submit to God's Order**: Respect biblical principles in worship, prioritizing Christ's headship over cultural trends. Whether in music, preaching, or fellowship, submit to God's design to strengthen the church's witness.

- **Examine Your Heart**: Before partaking in the Lord's Supper or worship, reflect on your motives and relationships (1 Corinthians 11:28). Reconcile with others, ensuring your worship unites the body and points to Christ's return.

## Prayer

*Father, we thank You for calling us to worship as Your fireproof church. Fill us with reverence for Your presence, love for Your body, and submission to Your order. Help us guard the Lord's Supper as a symbol of unity and hope, proclaiming Christ's death until He comes. Unite us as one, that we may glorify You in a fractured world. In Jesus' name,*

*Amen.*

# 12

## Diversity Without Division

### The Beauty of the Body

In the crucible of Corinth's pagan culture, the church stood as a radiant testimony to God's transforming grace. Yet, its diversity—rich with spiritual gifts and varied backgrounds—threatened to become a source of division rather than strength. In 1 Corinthians 12, the Apostle Paul confronts this challenge, presenting the church as the body of Christ, where every member, from the most prominent to the most hidden, is essential. The Corinthians, shaped by a city obsessed with status and self-promotion, were tempted to elevate certain gifts—tongues, prophecy, or wisdom—above others, creating hierarchies that fractured their witness. Paul's message is clear: diversity does not mean division. Just as a human body thrives through the coordinated work of its many parts, so the church must function as one body, united in Christ, with each member serving according to God's calling.

This chapter delves into 1 Corinthians 12, where Paul uses the vivid imagery of the body to call the church to embrace their diverse gifts while rejecting schisms. In a city like Corinth, where competition and individualism reigned, this call to unity was revolutionary. For churches today, the lesson is timeless: our differences—gifts, callings, and roles—are not obstacles but opportunities, designed by God to build a fireproof church that shines His glory in a divided world.

*Now concerning spiritual gifts, brethren, I would not have you ignorant. Ye know that ye were Gentiles, carried away unto these dumb idols, even as ye were led. Wherefore I give you to understand, that no man speaking by the Spirit of God calleth Jesus accursed: and that no man can say that Jesus is the Lord, but by the Holy Ghost. Now there are diversities of gifts, but the same Spirit. And there are differences of administrations, but the same Lord. And there are diversities of operations, but it is the same God which worketh all in all. But the manifestation of the Spirit is given to every man to profit withal. For to one is given by the Spirit the word of wisdom; to another the word of knowledge by the same Spirit; to another faith by the same Spirit; to another the gifts of healing by the same Spirit; to another the working of miracles; to another prophecy;*

*to another discerning of spirits; to another divers kinds of tongues; to another the interpretation of tongues: But all these worketh that one and the selfsame Spirit, dividing to every man severally as he will. For as the body is one, and hath many members, and all the members of that one body, being many, are one body: so also is Christ. For by one Spirit are we all baptized into one body, whether we be Jews or Gentiles, whether we be bond or free; and have been all made to drink into one Spirit. For the body is not one member, but many. If the foot shall say, Because I am not the hand, I am not of the body; is it therefore not of the body? And if the ear shall say, Because I am not the eye, I am not of the body; is it therefore not of the body? If the whole body were an eye, where were the hearing? If the whole were hearing, where were the smelling? But now hath God set the members every one of them in the body, as it hath pleased him. And if they were all one member, where were the body? But now are they many members, yet but one body. And the eye cannot say unto the hand, I have no need of thee: nor again the head to the feet, I have no need of you. Nay, much more those members of the body, which seem to be more feeble, are necessary: And those members of the body, which we think to be less honourable, upon these we bestow more abundant honour; and our uncomely parts have more abundant comeliness. For our comely parts have no need: but God hath tempered the body together, having given more abundant honour to that part which lacked. That there should be no schism in the body; but that the members should have the same care one for another. And whether one member suffer, all the members suffer with it; or one member be honoured, all the members rejoice with it. Now ye are the body of Christ, and members in particular. And God hath set some in the church, first apostles, secondarily prophets, thirdly teachers, after that miracles, then gifts of healings, helps, governments, diversities of tongues. Are all apostles? Are all prophets? Are all teachers? Are all workers of miracles? Have all the gifts of healing? Do all speak with tongues? Do all interpret? But covet earnestly the best gifts: and yet shew I unto you a more excellent way. (I Corinthians 12, KJV)*

# The Corinthian Context: From Idolatry to Unity

To grasp the power of Paul's teaching in 1 Corinthians 12, we must revisit the cultural furnace of Corinth, as explored in Chapter 1. Corinth was a thriving Roman colony, a hub of wealth, trade, and vice, situated on a narrow isthmus that funneled commerce across the Mediterranean. Its residents competed fiercely for status, recognition, and intellectual prowess, a culture vividly displayed in the Isthmian Games and the city's obsession with rhetoric and reputation. This spirit of one-upmanship seeped into the church, where believers began to rank their spiritual gifts, mirroring the social stratification of the city. A Roman citizen with the gift of wisdom might look down on a slave with the gift of helps, just as those with visible gifts like tongues sought prominence over those with quieter roles.

Paul begins by grounding the Corinthians in their spiritual transformation: "Ye know that ye were Gentiles, carried away unto these dumb idols, even as ye were led" (1 Corinthians 12:2, KJV). When he says 'dumb idols,' he doesn't mean stupid or ridiculous idols; he means idols that could not speak. They followed gods that could not give them direction or comfort or care, that could not impart to them wisdom and knowledge, that did not know the future, that could not help them in their time of need. These mute idols depended on their worshippers for everything—if an idol needed to be moved, they carried it; if it needed offerings, they provided them. That does seem pretty dumb, doesn't it? To dedicate your life to an idol, to worship something that cannot give you any sort of direction or peace, that depends upon you for everything.

The Corinthians were called from this ignorant worship to a living God who speaks through His Word, who is wise, powerful, and present. They turned from a diversity of idols—scattered across Corinth's temples and street corners—to a unity in Christ, called to worship the one true God as one body. They were called from a diversity of idols to a unity in Christ, and their worship was to be the worship of the one true God in one body. They were to leave behind the priorities and principles of the world and to follow the walk of Christ, and to have that same mind, as Paul tells us elsewhere, to have the mind of Christ. This shift was not just theological but countercultural, challenging the Corinthians to reject the divisive individualism of their city and embrace the unity of Christ's body.

## The Body of Christ: Unity in Diversity

Paul's central metaphor in 1 Corinthians 12 is the body of Christ, a powerful illustration of how diversity serves unity. Let's read the passage:

> *"Now concerning spiritual gifts, brethren, I would not have you ignorant. Ye know that ye were Gentiles, carried away unto these dumb idols, even as ye were led. Wherefore I give you to understand, that no man speaking by the Spirit of God calleth Jesus accursed: and that no man can say that Jesus is the Lord, but*

by the Holy Ghost. Now there are diversities of
gifts, but the same Spirit. And there are
differences of administrations, but the same
Lord. And there are diversities of operations,
but it is the same God which worketh all in all.
But the manifestation of the Spirit is given to
every man to profit withal. For to one is given
by the Spirit the word of wisdom; to another the
word of knowledge by the same Spirit; to
another faith by the same Spirit; to another the
gifts of healing by the same Spirit; to another
the working of miracles; to another prophecy;
to another discerning of spirits; to another
divers kinds of tongues; to another the
interpretation of tongues: but all these worketh
that one and the selfsame Spirit, dividing to
every man severally as he will. For as the body
is one, and hath many members, and all the
members of that one body, being many, are
one body: so also is Christ. For by one Spirit
are we all baptized into one body, whether we
be Jews or Gentiles, whether we be bond or
free; and have been all made to drink into one
Spirit. For the body is not one member, but
many. If the foot shall say, Because I am not
the hand, I am not of the body; is it therefore
not of the body? And if the ear shall say,
Because I am not the eye, I am not of the
body; is it therefore not of the body? If the
whole body were an eye, where were the

*hearing? If the whole were hearing, where were the smelling? But now hath God set the members every one of them in the body, as it hath pleased him. And if they were all one member, where were the body? But now are they many members, yet but one body. And the eye cannot say unto the hand, I have no need of thee: nor again the head to the feet, I have no need of you. Nay, much more those members of the body, which seem to be more feeble, are necessary: and those members of the body, which we think to be less honourable, upon these we bestow more abundant honour; and our uncomely parts have more abundant comeliness. For our comely parts have no need: but God hath tempered the body together, having given more abundant honour to that part which lacked: that there should be no schism in the body; but that the members should have the same care one for another. And whether one member suffer, all the members suffer with it; or one member be honoured, all the members rejoice with it. Now ye are the body of Christ, and members in particular. And God hath set some in the church, first apostles, secondarily prophets, thirdly teachers, after that miracles, then gifts of healings, helps, governments, diversities of tongues. Are all apostles? Are all prophets? Are all teachers? Are all workers of miracles?*

*Have all the gifts of healing? Do all speak with tongues? Do all interpret? But covet earnestly the best gifts: and yet shew I unto you a more excellent way." (1 Corinthians 12:1–31, KJV)*

Paul anchors the church's identity in their shared salvation: "For by one Spirit are we all baptized into one body, whether we be Jews or Gentiles, whether we be bond or free; and have been all made to drink into one Spirit" (1 Corinthians 12:13, KJV). Our baptism is a symbol of the old man passing away, that the old man is buried with Christ in His death, but a new life is being lived as we are raised to walk in a newness of life. This new life began when Christ emerged from the tomb in a new kind of body, with a life that had never existed before. That's the life that He has implanted in us, and we are His body here on earth. Our old egos, desires, and priorities are buried; we now share the mind of Christ.

This shared mind is the foundation of unity. If I have the mind of Christ, and if you have the mind of Christ, then we're all going to be thinking the same things, aren't we? We're all going to be having the same priorities, the same direction, the same desires. Yet, this unity does not erase diversity. Paul lists various gifts—wisdom, knowledge, faith, healing, miracles, prophecy, discerning of spirits, tongues, and interpretation—all given by the same Spirit, distributed as He wills. Christians are not cookie-cutter people.

We don't all exactly resemble one another. We don't all have the same gifts, the same qualities, the same capabilities. We don't all have the same calling or the same place or purpose.

## The Body's Harmony: Every Part Essential

Paul's body analogy is both practical and profound. He asks, "If the foot shall say, Because I am not the hand, I am not of the body; is it therefore not of the body? And if the ear shall say, Because I am not the eye, I am not of the body; is it therefore not of the body?" (1 Corinthians 12:15–16, KJV). The answer is clear: every part belongs, regardless of its role. The eye doesn't say to the hand, 'I have no need of you.' As a matter of fact, eye-hand coordination is something that we value greatly, isn't it? The head needs the feet to move; the feet need the head to stay focused.

Every part is essential, and when one part hurts, every part of your body knows it. When one part is honored, every part of your body feels the pleasure of the compliment."

This interdependence counters Corinth's competitive culture. Some believers, perhaps those with visible gifts like tongues, saw themselves as superior, while others, with quieter roles like helpers or governments, felt insignificant.

Paul corrects this: "Nay, much more those members of the body, which seem to be more feeble, are necessary" (1 Corinthians 12:22, KJV). The parts we don't see are the parts that work the hardest, aren't they? Your heart never takes a break. It beats day in, day out, moment by moment. Your inward parts are constantly working; they never get to rest. The hardest-working parts, the most vital parts, are the ones that nobody notices. The church must honor these "inward parts"—those who serve quietly in prayer, administration, or mercy—as vital to the body's health.

Paul's goal is clear: "That there should be no schism in the body; but that the members should have the same care one for another" (1 Corinthians 12:25, KJV). The Greek word *schisma* echoes the "divisions" (*schismata*) from 1 Corinthians 1:10, linking this chapter to the broader theme of unity. We don't separate or pull ourselves apart because of our differences, and we don't evaluate ourselves by the different giftings and purposes that God has put in our lives, because every part of the body is necessary.

# The Corinthian Church: A Diverse Yet Unified Witness

The Corinthian church was a radical social experiment, uniting Roman citizens, Greek freedmen, and slaves in one body. This diversity was a testament to the gospel's power, as seen in converts like Crispus, the synagogue leader, and Gaius, a Roman nobleman (Chapter 1). Yet, it also posed challenges. A Roman citizen might have struggled to serve alongside a slave, just as someone with the gift of prophecy might have looked down on one with the gift of helps. Paul insists that all are baptized into one body by one Spirit, transcending social and cultural divides. We are all called together in a diversity of skill and interests and personalities and social position and gifts. We are all together to work together.

Paul's rhetorical questions—"Are all apostles? Are all prophets? Are all teachers?" (1 Corinthians 12:29, KJV)—remind the Corinthians that no single gift defines the church. Each member has a role, and none can say to another, "I have no need of you." This was countercultural in Corinth, where status and visibility were everything. You may say, "Well, my place is in a place of distinction. I'm not the nose; nobody ever sees me." But that's okay, because the parts that are inside are the ones we take care of the most, aren't they? Our heart and our innards, they're vitally important.

# Conclusion: A Unified Body in a Divided World

The Corinthian church, despite its flaws, was a powerful testament to God's ability to unite diverse believers into one body. In a city that thrived on division and self-promotion, Paul called them to a higher standard: a church where every member, from the most visible to the most hidden, serves together in the mind of Christ. Whatever God has called you to, whatever gifting He has given you, whatever purpose He has placed upon you, let us serve in unity together. A fireproof church is one that reflects this unity, shining as a beacon of Christ's love in a fractured world. As we continue through 1 Corinthians, may we learn from Paul's call to embrace our diversity without division, building a church that glorifies Christ alone.

# Application: Building a Fireproof Church Through Unity

A fireproof church embraces its diversity while rejecting division, reflecting the harmony of Christ's body. Here are four ways to apply Paul's teaching in 1 Corinthians 12:

- **Value Every Gift**: Recognize that every gift— whether visible like prophecy or quiet like helps— is given by the same Spirit for the body's benefit.

Whatever your gift, whatever your purpose, we aren't following dumb idols that divide us and call us to different purposes. Honor those who serve in unseen roles, knowing they are vital to the church's health.

- **Reject Comparison**: Avoid comparing your gifts or roles to others', as this breeds pride or insecurity. Paul's body analogy reminds us, "If the whole body were an eye, where were the hearing?" (1 Corinthians 12:17, KJV). Embrace your calling, trusting God's design.

- **Care for One Another**: When one member suffers, all suffer; when one is honored, all rejoice (1 Corinthians 12:26, KJV). As I said, "We work together. We coordinate together. We serve one another. We care for one another, and we find each other to be important." Build a church where every member is valued and supported.

- **Pursue the Mind of Christ**: Unity comes from sharing Christ's priorities and direction. As I noted, "If you have the mind of Christ, then we're all going to be moving in the same direction." Study God's Word to align with His will, fostering harmony despite differences (Philippians 2:5, KJV).

## Prayer

*Father, we are so thankful that You have placed us together in a body, and that we're not out here all by ourselves, trying to live out Christ in a world that hates Him and having to do it all on our own. Lord, we pray that You will knit us in love, that our diverse gifts will strengthen our unity, and that we will serve as one body, reflecting Your glory. In Jesus' name, we pray,*

*Amen.*

# 13

## Called to Love: A More Excellent Way

### Introduction: The Heart of a Fireproof Church

The Corinthian church, born in a city of wealth and pride, was richly gifted yet deeply divided. As explored in previous chapters, their competitive culture fueled disputes over personalities, morality, and spiritual gifts, threatening their witness as Christ's body. In 1 Corinthians 13, Paul offers a transformative solution: a way of life that surpasses the gifts they valued so highly. Often read at weddings for its poetic beauty, this chapter is far more than a sentimental reflection on love. It is a convicting call to embrace agape love—God's selfless, sacrificial love—as the foundation of a unified church. This love, Paul argues, is the "more excellent way" that binds believers together, transcending temporary gifts and enduring for eternity.

This chapter explores 1 Corinthians 13, where Paul redirects the Corinthians from their pursuit of spiritual prominence to the supremacy of love. In a city obsessed with status and self-exaltation, this message was revolutionary. For churches today, it remains a vital call to build a fireproof church, one that rejects ego and embraces Christ's love as its cornerstone.

## The Corinthian Context: A Church Fractured by Pride

Corinth, as detailed in Chapter 1, was a thriving Roman colony, a hub of commerce and vice where competition defined every aspect of life. Residents vied for recognition in the marketplace, the forum, and the Isthmian Games, seeking status through wealth, rhetoric, or public acclaim. This spirit of one-upmanship infiltrated the church, leading to conflicts over favorite preachers (1 Corinthians 1:10–12), moral compromises (1 Corinthians 5:1–2), and the celebration of the Lord's Supper (1 Corinthians 11:17–22). A significant source of division was the Corinthians' misuse of spiritual gifts. They treated gifts like tongues, prophecy, and healing as badges of personal superiority, competing to outshine one another in a manner that echoed their city's culture.

Before their conversion, the Corinthians worshipped mute idols—lifeless gods that offered no guidance or comfort, requiring worshippers to carry their burdens. As believers, they were called to a new way of life, united in Christ as one body. Yet, their old habits persisted, turning God's gifts into tools for self-promotion. Like the disciples who rejoiced in their power over demons rather than their salvation (Luke 10:17–20), the Corinthians focused on the spectacle of their gifts rather than their purpose: to edify the church. Paul seeks to correct this, urging them to pursue a way that far surpasses their prideful priorities.

## The More Excellent Way: The Supremacy of Love

Paul concludes Chapter 12 by encouraging the Corinthians to desire the best spiritual gifts while pointing them to a higher path: "Covet earnestly the best gifts: and yet shew I unto you a more excellent way" (1 Corinthians 12:31, KJV). He then delivers the timeless words of 1 Corinthians 13:

> *"Though I speak with the tongues of men and of angels, and have not charity, I am become as sounding brass, or a tinkling cymbal. And though I have the gift of prophecy, and understand all mysteries, and all knowledge; and though I have all faith, so that I could remove mountains, and have not charity, I am nothing. And though I bestow all my goods to feed the poor, and though I give my body to be burned, and have not charity, it profi⬚tes me nothing. Charity suffereth long, and is kind;*

*charity envieth not; charity vaunteth not itself, is not puffed up, doth not behave itself unseemly, seeketh not her own, is not easily provoked, thinketh no evil; rejoiceth not in iniquity, but rejoiceth in the truth; beareth all things, believeth all things, hopeth all things, endureth all things. Charity never faileth: but whether there be prophecies, they shall fail; whether there be tongues, they shall cease; whether there be knowledge, it shall vanish away. For we know in part, and we prophesy in part. But when that which is perfect is come, then that which is in part shall be done away. When I was a child, I spake as a child, I understood as a child, I thought as a child: but when I became a man, I put away childish things. For now we see through a glass, darkly; but then face to face: now I know in part; but then shall I know even as also I am known. And now abideth faith, hope, charity, these three; but the greatest of these is charity." (1 Corinthians 13:1–13, KJV)*

Paul redefines the value of spiritual gifts, emphasizing that without love, they are worthless. Speaking in tongues, even if it were as eloquent as angelic speech, becomes mere noise—like the grating clang of cymbals—if not rooted in love. Such speech repels rather than attracts others to the gospel. Similarly, the gift of prophecy, the ability to understand divine mysteries, or faith strong enough to move mountains amounts to nothing if exercised without love. Even sacrificial acts, like giving all one's possessions to the poor or offering one's body as a martyr, are profitless if driven by pride or self-interest rather than love. In Corinth, where believers often performed good deeds to gain recognition, this was a radical challenge. Acts of charity done for personal validation or to feel good feed the ego, drawing us away from God rather than toward Him.

## The Nature of *Agape* Love

Paul describes love with attributes that directly oppose Corinth's self-centered culture: "Charity suffereth long, and is kind; charity envieth not; charity vaunteth not itself, is not puffed up, doth not behave itself unseemly, seeketh not her own, is not easily provoked, thinketh no evil; rejoiceth not in iniquity, but rejoiceth in the truth; beareth all things, believeth all things, hopeth all things, endureth all things" (1 Corinthians 13:4–7, KJV). This agape love, translated as "charity" in the KJV, reflects God's selfless love— giving without expecting anything in return, as God gave His Son for an undeserving world (John 3:16).

Love is the basic, defining character trait of the Christian life. Jesus said, "By this all will know that you are My disciples, if you have love for one another." (John 13:35).

The identifying characteristic of a disciple of Jesus Christ is love. In my own nature, my highest desire and driving motivation is to be loved. We begin as infants and through all stages of life we seek to be wanted, included, cared for.

A life spent seeking love leads to frustration and disappointment. The spiritual life begins with laying aside my desires and seeking to love others, regardless of return.

Greek, the language of the New Testament, has 4 different words for love. The word Paul uses in this passage means an unselfish, sacrificial love. It is the word that is used for how God loves us.

Every other kind of love comes with expectations. Romantic love, family love, friendship love — all must be returned in order to be complete. Loving someone in one of these ways without being loved in return leads to heartache, bitterness, and broken relationships.

*Agape* love, Godly love, is self-fulfilling. The completion of loving someone in this way is not in them loving you back, but in you getting to experience the way God loves you personally and deeply. In Romans 5:8, Paul gives us a breathtaking picture of God's infinite, undemanding love — "But God demonstrates His own love toward us, in that while we were still sinners, Christ died for us." God displayed His love for us by Christ giving His life for those who continued to sin. He loved us while we hated Him.

John 3:16 tells us that God loved and sacrificed for all, knowing many would never accept or return His love. This is why the doctrine of limited atonement is dangerous – it diminishes the self-sufficiency of God's love. The fact that there are those in Hell for whom Christ died does not diminish Christ's efficacy, it magnifies God's magnanimity. Real love, God's love, the love of God's people produced by the Holy Spirit in the new nature, is complete in the giving.

In Corinth, where envy and boasting were rampant, love's patience and kindness required enduring difficult people without resentment. Love does not flaunt itself or seek recognition, rejecting the city's obsession with status. It treats others with respect, refusing to act rudely or demand its own way. Unlike the world's love, which seeks personal gain—even in relationships like parenting or marriage—agape love serves others without expecting reciprocation. It avoids quick offense, assumes the best of others rather than the worst, and confronts sin while celebrating truth.

This love endures like a Roman arch, a marvel of engineering that has stood for millennia across the ancient world. A Roman arch is constructed of carefully shaped stones, each pressing against its neighbor to form a curved structure. At its apex sits the keystone, a uniquely angled stone that locks the entire arch in place. Without the keystone, the arch would collapse under its own weight, but with it, the stones are pressed together, their mutual dependence creating strength. Remarkably, the more weight placed upon the arch—whether from the passage of time, the tread of countless feet, or the burdens of nature—the stronger it becomes, as the pressure drives the stones closer together, reinforcing their unity. So it is with agape love in the church. Christ, our keystone, holds us together, binding diverse believers into one body. The pressures of trials, conflicts, or differences do not weaken this love; rather, they strengthen it, as Christ's presence presses us closer to one another, forging a unity that endures. Just as Roman arches like the Pont du Gard or the aqueducts of Rome have withstood centuries, the church, united by Christ's love, stands firm through the ages, a testament to the enduring power of *agape* love.

In the Greek and biblical understanding, love is not a fleeting emotion but a deliberate choice, rooted in the heart as the seat of the will. Unlike our modern view, where the heart is associated with feelings and romance, the Greeks saw the heart (*kardia*) as the center of decision-making, where choices and commitments are formed. The bowels (*splagchna*), often translated as "compassion" or "affections" in Scripture (e.g., Philippians 1:8, KJV), were the seat of deep emotions—grief, longing, or pity. The mind (*nous*), meanwhile, was the organ of imagination and understanding, where thoughts and ideas take shape. For the Corinthians, steeped in this worldview, Paul's call to love was a call to align their wills with God's, choosing to prioritize others above themselves. C.S. Lewis, in The Abolition of Man, captures the danger of neglecting this balance: "We make men without chests and expect of them virtue and enterprise. We laugh at honour and are shocked to find traitors in our midst." Lewis's "chest" aligns with the biblical heart, the seat of moral courage and decision, without which emotions and intellect produce hollow actions. Just as God chose to love an unworthy world by giving His Son (John 3:16), believers are called to make the conscious decision to love, not because of emotional warmth or intellectual approval, but because their heart—the core of their will—commits to reflecting Christ's selfless love. This choice, grounded in the heart, enables the church to embody agape, serving one another in a way that mirrors the unity of a Roman arch, where every stone, held by the keystone, contributes to an enduring whole.

## The Permanence of Love

Paul contrasts the temporary nature of spiritual gifts with the eternal endurance of love: "Charity never faileth: but whether there be prophecies, they shall fail; whether there be tongues, they shall cease;

whether there be knowledge, it shall vanish away" (1 Corinthians 13:8, KJV). In the early church, when the New Testament was incomplete—perhaps only the Gospel of Mark or Galatians circulated—gifts like prophecy and tongues were vital, providing fragmented glimpses of God's will. These revelations were like seeing "through a glass, darkly" (1 Corinthians 13:12, KJV), a reference to the cloudy, distorted reflection offered by ancient mirrors, often made of polished metal. Such mirrors, unlike modern glass, produced dim, imperfect images, much like the partial and fleeting revelations of prophecy or tongues. These gifts were necessary in the church's infancy, when believers lacked a complete written revelation, but they were temporary, designed to cease when the full truth was revealed. Paul explains, "For we know in part, and we prophesy in part. But when that which is perfect is come, then that which is in part shall be done away" (1 Corinthians 13:9–10, KJV). The "perfect" here is not an eschatological reference to Christ's return, as some suppose, but the completed Word of God—the full canon of Scripture. With the Bible's completion, believers no longer rely on fragmented utterances but can know God's will clearly, as if seeing "face to face" (1 Corinthians 13:12, KJV). This phrase evokes the intimate, direct encounter of Moses with God (Exodus 33:11), signifying the clarity and sufficiency of Scripture. Today, we have the privilege of knowing God through His Word, a revelation so complete that it allows us to understand His will as clearly as one person knows another in direct conversation, far surpassing the cloudy glimpses of the early church's prophetic gifts. Love, however, endures beyond these temporary aids, remaining alongside faith and hope as a permanent gift, with charity as the greatest, for it binds the church together in Christ's image.

Paul uses the analogy of maturity: "When I was a child, I spake as a child, I understood as a child, I thought as a child: but when I became a man, I put away childish things" (1 Corinthians 13:11, KJV). The early church, in its infancy, relied on these temporary gifts, but with the mature revelation of Scripture, they were set aside. Love, however, remains, alongside faith and hope. Of these, love is the greatest, for it carries others with us, sustaining the church through trials and uniting us in Christ's image.

## Conclusion: The Greatest Gift

In a city driven by pride and division, Paul called the Corinthians to a more excellent way: the way of love. This agape love, modeled on God's selfless gift of His Son, transforms a fractured church into a unified body, reflecting Christ's glory. A fireproof church chooses love over ego, service over status, and Scripture over worldly wisdom. As we continue through 1 Corinthians, may we embrace this enduring gift of love, building a church that glorifies Christ alone.

# Application: Building a Fireproof Church Through Love

A fireproof church embodies the agape love of 1 Corinthians 13, choosing to serve selflessly despite differences or challenges. Here are four ways to apply Paul's teaching:

- **Prioritize Love Over Pride:** Use your gifts to build up the church, not to exalt yourself. Whether your role is visible or hidden, let love guide your actions, ensuring they draw others to Christ rather than to you.

- **Choose Selfless Service:** Make the deliberate choice to put others first, even when it's difficult or unreciprocated. Like God's love for us, serve without expecting reward, trusting that such love reflects Christ's image.

- **Live Out Love's Qualities:** Practice patience, kindness, humility, and endurance in your relationships. Confront sin with truth, assume the best of others, and treat all with respect, countering the world's self-centered culture.

- **Anchor in God's Word:** Immerse yourself in the completed Scriptures, which reveal God's will clearly. Let the Bible guide your love, providing the wisdom to live out agape love in every circumstance.

# Prayer

*Father, we thank You for the gift of Your love, poured into us through Christ. Direct our wills to choose love for one another, that we may be conduits of Your grace. Build us into a fireproof church, united in Your truth and reflecting Your glory. In Jesus' name,*

*Amen.*

# 14

## Orderly Worship for the Edification of All

### A Church That Builds Up

In the bustling, competitive city of Corinth, the church faced a persistent challenge: a desire for personal prominence that threatened its unity. As explored in previous chapters, the Corinthians' cultural obsession with status led to divisions over preachers, morality, and spiritual gifts (1 Corinthians 1:10–12; 5:1–2; 12:1–31). In 1 Corinthians 14, Paul addresses their chaotic worship practices, particularly their misuse of tongues, which they prized for its spectacle rather than its service to the body. He calls them to pursue love and prioritize gifts that edify the church, especially prophecy, which communicates God's truth clearly. In a city where self-exaltation reigned, Paul's insistence on orderly, intelligible worship was revolutionary, redirecting the church toward mutual strengthening rather than individual display.

This chapter delves into 1 Corinthians 14, where Paul instructs the Corinthians to channel their zeal for spiritual gifts into practices that build up the body. For churches today, this message is a timeless call to worship in a way that glorifies God and edifies all, creating a fireproof church united in love and truth.

## The Corinthian Context: Chaos in Worship

As detailed in Chapter 1, Corinth was a Roman colony defined by commerce, vice, and competition. Its residents sought recognition through wealth, rhetoric, and public displays, a mindset that infiltrated the church. Unlike modern congregations, where participation can be minimal, the Corinthian believers were eager to take center stage, each vying to showcase their spiritual gifts.

This led to disorderly worship gatherings, where multiple voices—some speaking in tongues, others prophesying—created confusion rather than clarity. These gatherings, often held after sundown due to work schedules, were more like family reunions than structured services, with believers sharing songs, teachings, or revelations. However, their competitive spirit turned these moments into opportunities for self-promotion, echoing the city's culture of one-upmanship.

The Corinthians' fascination with tongues stemmed from their cultural context, where dramatic displays were valued. Yet, these gifts were misunderstood. Tongues, as seen in Acts 2, were known languages used to proclaim the gospel to diverse audiences, not unintelligible babbling.

The Corinthians, however, used them to elevate themselves, creating a spectacle that left others confused and unedified. Paul, having experienced the proper use of tongues in his missionary journeys, seeks to correct this misuse, urging the church to focus on gifts that strengthen the body and reflect God's order.

## The Priority of Prophecy: Edifying the Church

Paul begins 1 Corinthians 14 with a clear directive: "Follow after charity, and desire spiritual gifts, but rather that ye may prophesy" (1 Corinthians 14:1, KJV). He contrasts tongues with prophecy, emphasizing their differing impacts:

> "For he that speaketh in an unknown tongue speaketh not unto men, but unto God: for no man understandeth him; howbeit in the spirit he speaketh mysteries. But he that prophesieth speaketh unto men to edification, and exhortation, and comfort. He that speaketh in

*an unknown tongue edifieth himself; but he that prophesieth edifieth the church. I would that ye all spake with tongues, but rather that ye prophesied: for greater is he that prophesieth than he that speaketh with tongues, except he interpret, that the church may receive edifying."*
*(1 Corinthians 14:2–5, KJV)*

Tongues, when uninterpreted, are unintelligible, speaking mysteries that benefit no one but the speaker. Prophecy, however, builds up the church through clear teaching, encouragement, and consolation. In the early church, before the New Testament was complete, prophecy involved direct revelations from God. Today, with the full Scriptures, prophecy is the proclamation of God's Word, sharing its truths in a way that others can understand.

Paul's preference for prophecy reflects its ability to edify the entire body, unlike tongues, which, without interpretation, serve only the individual, fostering pride rather than unity.

Paul illustrates this with practical analogies: "And even things without life giving sound, whether pipe or harp, except they give a distinction in the sounds, how shall it be known what is piped or harped? For if the trumpet give an uncertain sound, who shall prepare himself to the battle?" (1 Corinthians 14:7–8, KJV). Just as a flute or trumpet must produce clear notes to convey meaning, speech in the church must be understandable to benefit others.

Uninterpreted tongues are like speaking into the air, meaningless to listeners, much like a foreign language to an outsider (1 Corinthians 14:10–11).

## Tongues as a Sign for Unbelievers

Paul clarifies the purpose of tongues by referencing their use in Acts 2 and citing Isaiah: "In the law it is written, With men of other tongues and other lips will I speak unto this people; and yet for all that will they not hear me, saith the Lord. Wherefore tongues are for a sign, not to them that believe, but to them that believe not: but prophesying serveth not for them that believe not, but for them which believe" (1 Corinthians 14:21–22, KJV, citing Isaiah 28:11–12). On the Day of Pentecost, tongues enabled the disciples to proclaim the gospel to Jews from diverse regions, each hearing in their native language (Acts 2:5–11). This miraculous sign validated the gospel for unbelieving Jews, fulfilling Isaiah's prophecy that God would speak through foreign tongues to a stubborn people. Similarly, in Acts 10 and 19, tongues confirmed the inclusion of Gentiles and John's disciples in the church, signaling God's universal grace.

Paul's statement, "I would that ye all spake with tongues" (1 Corinthians 14:5, KJV), reflects his missionary experience, where tongues enabled him to share the gospel with those who spoke different languages. However, in the Corinthian church, where tongues were used to show off rather than evangelize, they caused confusion. Paul insists that tongues must be interpreted to edify the church: "If any man speak in an unknown tongue, let it be by two, or at the most by three, and that by course; and let one interpret. But if there be no interpreter, let him keep silence in the church; and let him speak to himself, and to God" (1 Corinthians 14:27–28, KJV).

## Orderly Worship: Unity in Spirit and Truth

Paul emphasizes that worship must engage both spirit and mind: "What is it then? I will pray with the spirit, and I will pray with the understanding also: I will sing with the spirit, and I will sing with the understanding also" (1 Corinthians 14:15, KJV). Unintelligible tongues disengage the mind, producing worship that lacks truth, contrary to Jesus' teaching that true worshipers worship "in spirit and in truth" (John 4:24, KJV). Paul warns that if an outsider hears uninterpreted tongues, "will they not say that ye are mad?" (1 Corinthians 14:23, KJV). In contrast, clear prophecy convicts unbelievers, revealing the secrets of their hearts and leading them to worship God (1 Corinthians 14:24–25).

To ensure edification, Paul provides practical guidelines: "How is it then, brethren? When ye come together, everyone of you hath a psalm, hath a doctrine, hath a tongue, hath a revelation, hath an interpretation. Let all things be done unto edifying" (1 Corinthians 14:26, KJV).

Worship should involve participation from all, but it must be orderly, with only two or three speaking in tongues or prophesying, each in turn, and always with interpretation or evaluation. This reflects God's character: "For God is not the author of confusion, but of peace, as in all churches of the saints" (1 Corinthians 14:33, KJV).

Paul addresses a specific issue of disorder: "Let your women keep silence in the churches: for it is not permitted unto them to speak; but they are commanded to be under obedience, as also saith the law" (1 Corinthians 14:34, KJV). In Corinth's cultural context, where women's public speaking could be seen as disruptive, Paul calls for submission to maintain order, suggesting questions be addressed privately to avoid chaos. This instruction, rooted in the church's need for clarity, does not diminish women's value but aligns with the goal of edifying worship.

## The Sufficiency of Scripture

The temporary nature of certain gifts, like tongues and prophecy as direct revelation, underscores the sufficiency of the completed Scriptures. As discussed in Chapter 13, gifts like tongues ceased with the completion of the New Testament, which provides all we need for life and godliness (2 Peter 1:3, KJV). Today, prophecy is not receiving new revelations but proclaiming God's Word, enabling every believer to share its truths with others. Paul's call to "be not children in understanding" (1 Corinthians 14:20, KJV) urges the church to mature in its use of gifts, focusing on what builds up the body rather than what exalts the individual.

## Conclusion: A Unified Witness in Worship

In a city driven by competition and chaos, Paul called the Corinthians to a worship that reflects God's order and love. By prioritizing prophecy over tongues, engaging both spirit and mind, and maintaining order, the church becomes a beacon of God's presence, convicting unbelievers and strengthening believers. A fireproof church worships in a way that edifies all, grounded in the completed Word of God. As we continue through 1 Corinthians, may we embrace this call to orderly worship, building a church that glorifies Christ alone.

## Application: Building a Fireproof Church Through Orderly Worship

A fireproof church worships in a way that prioritizes edification, clarity, and order, reflecting God's character. Here are four ways to apply Paul's teaching in 1 Corinthians 14:

- Pursue Love in Worship: Actively seek opportunities to love others by using your gifts to build up the church, not yourself. Let love guide every song, teaching, or sharing, ensuring it serves the body.

- Prioritize Clarity: Share God's Word in a way that others can understand, whether teaching a neighbor or encouraging a friend. Avoid practices that confuse or exclude, focusing on clear proclamation of Scripture.

- Engage Spirit and Mind: Worship with both heartfelt devotion and clear understanding, as Jesus taught (John 4:24). Ensure your prayers and praises are intelligible, uniting the congregation in truth.

- Maintain Order: Foster a worship environment where all can participate, but in an orderly manner. Evaluate teachings against Scripture, and ensure every contribution strengthens the church.

# Prayer

*Father, we thank You for Your complete Word, which equips us for life and godliness. Help us to pursue love, share Your truth clearly, and worship in spirit and truth, that our church may be a unified witness to Your glory. In Jesus' name,*

*Amen.*

# 15

## A Call to Unity: The Hope of the Resurrection

### The Gospel That Saves

In the vibrant, prideful city of Corinth, the church faced challenges that threatened its unity and witness: divisions over leaders, moral failures, and chaotic worship, as explored in previous chapters. In 1 Corinthians 15, Paul confronts a deeper issue—doubts about the resurrection of the dead—that struck at the heart of the Christian faith.

Some Corinthians, influenced by their Greco-Roman culture, questioned whether the dead could rise, a skepticism that undermined the gospel itself. Paul responds by reaffirming the gospel he preached: Christ's death, burial, and resurrection according to the Scriptures. This gospel, the foundation of salvation, offers not only forgiveness but also the hope of a resurrected body, free from sin and death. For a church tempted by self-exaltation, this message redirects focus to Christ's victory and the promise of eternal life.

This chapter explores 1 Corinthians 15, where Paul defends the resurrection's reality and its implications for believers. For churches today, it is a call to stand firm in the gospel, living with the assurance of resurrection and abounding in God's work, building a fireproof church anchored in hope.

## The Corinthian Context: A Culture Skeptical of Resurrection

Corinth, as described in Chapter 1, was a hub of commerce and competition, where status and spectacle dominated. Its Greco-Roman culture often viewed the body as inferior to the soul, with philosophers like Plato teaching that death freed the soul from the body's prison. This worldview led some Corinthians to deny the resurrection of the dead (1 Corinthians 15:12), seeing it as unnecessary or impossible. Such skepticism echoed broader Greco-Roman thought, where bodily resurrection was a foreign concept, unlike the Jewish hope rooted in Scriptures like Job and Psalms. The Corinthians' competitive spirit, seen in their disputes over gifts and leaders, likely amplified these doubts, as some sought to appear intellectually superior by rejecting bodily resurrection.

Paul, aware of these cultural influences, addresses the church as a missionary who once persecuted believers but was transformed by encountering the risen Christ (1 Corinthians 15:8–10). His personal testimony underscores the gospel's power to change lives, calling the Corinthians to cling to the truth they received rather than the philosophies of their culture.

## The Gospel: Christ's Death, Burial, and Resurrection

Paul begins by clarifying the gospel: "Moreover, brethren, I declare unto you the gospel which I preached unto you, which also ye have received, and wherein ye stand; By which also ye are saved, if ye keep in memory what I preached unto you, unless ye have believed in vain. For I delivered unto you first of all that which I also received, how that Christ died for our sins according to the scriptures; And that he was buried, and that he rose again the third day according to the scriptures" (1 Corinthians 15:1–4, KJV). The gospel is not merely Christ's death but His atoning, substitutionary death for our sins, fulfilling Old Testament prophecies (e.g., Isaiah 53:5). His burial confirms His death's reality, and His resurrection on the third day validates His victory over sin, as foretold in Scriptures like Psalm 16:10.

Paul supports this with eyewitness testimony: "And that he was seen of Cephas, then of the twelve: After that, he was seen of above five hundred brethren at once; of whom the greater part remain unto this present, but some are fallen asleep. After that, he was seen of James; then of all the apostles. And last of all he was seen of me also, as of one born out of due time" (1 Corinthians 15:5–8, KJV). These witnesses—Peter, the apostles, over 500 believers, James, and Paul himself—provide undeniable evidence, as many were still alive and could be questioned by the Corinthians. Unlike myths, the resurrection was attested by hundreds who saw, touched, and ate with the risen Christ (Luke 24:39–43), refuting claims of fabrication. The apostles gained no worldly wealth or honor; most faced persecution and martyrdom, yet held fast to this truth, a testament to its reality.

## The Necessity of the Resurrection

Paul confronts the Corinthians' denial head-on: "Now if Christ be preached that he rose from the dead, how say some among you that there is no resurrection of the dead? But if there be no resurrection of the dead, then is Christ not risen: And if Christ be not risen, then is our preaching vain, and your faith is also vain" (1 Corinthians 15:12–14, KJV). If the dead cannot rise, Christ did not rise, rendering the gospel empty and believers' faith futile. Without the resurrection, Christians are false witnesses, still in their sins, and those who died in Christ are lost (1 Corinthians 15:15–18). Paul declares, "And if in this life only we have hope in Christ, we are of all men most miserable" (1 Corinthians 15:19, KJV). The resurrection is the cornerstone of salvation, without which Christianity collapses.

Yet Paul affirms, "But now is Christ risen from the dead, and become the firstfruits of them that slept" (1 Corinthians 15:20, KJV). Christ's resurrection is the firstfruits, the initial harvest guaranteeing the full resurrection of believers. As death entered through Adam, resurrection comes through Christ, the last Adam: "For as in Adam all die, even so in Christ shall all be made alive" (1 Corinthians 15:22, KJV).

This hope extends to all who belong to Christ, who will be raised at His coming, when He delivers the kingdom to the Father, having defeated all enemies, including death (1 Corinthians 15:23–26).

## The Nature of the Resurrection Body

Paul addresses a practical question: "But some man will say, How are the dead raised up? and with what body do they come?" (1 Corinthians 15:35, KJV). He responds with an analogy: "Thou fool, that which thou sowest is not quickened, except it die: And that which thou sowest, thou sowest not that body that shall be, but bare grain, it may chance of wheat, or of some other grain: But God giveth it a body as it hath pleased him, and to every seed his own body" (1 Corinthians 15:36–38, KJV). Just as a seed is buried and transformed into a stalk, the body we bury is not the one raised. The sown body is perishable, dishonored, and weak; the raised body is imperishable, glorious, and powerful, a spiritual body suited for eternity (1 Corinthians 15:42–44).

Paul contrasts earthly and heavenly bodies: "As is the earthy, such are they also that are earthy: and as is the heavenly, such are they also that are heavenly. And as we have borne the image of the earthy, we shall also bear the image of the heavenly" (1 Corinthians 15:47–49, KJV). The first Adam was earthly, made of dust; Christ, the second Adam, is heavenly, a life-giving spirit. Our resurrection bodies will reflect Christ's, free from disease, decay, or sin, able to appear, eat, or ascend as He did (Luke 24:41–43; Acts 1:9). As 1 John 3:2 promises, we will be like Him when we see Him as He is, transformed into His likeness.

## The Mystery of Transformation

Paul unveils a profound truth: "Behold, I shew you a mystery; We shall not all sleep, but we shall all be changed, In a moment, in the twinkling of an eye, at the last trump: for the trumpet shall sound, and the dead shall be raised incorruptible, and we shall be changed" (1 Corinthians 15:51–52, KJV). In Scripture, a "mystery" (*musterion*) is not a puzzle to be solved but a divine truth previously hidden, now revealed by

God's Spirit through His apostles. Unlike Old Testament saints, who grasped the hope of resurrection (e.g., Job 19:26; Psalm 16:10), the specifics of how believers would receive glorified bodies—whether dead or alive—remained veiled. Paul now discloses this mystery: not all believers will die ("sleep"), but all, whether living or dead, will be instantly transformed at Christ's return. This event, often called the rapture, marks the culmination of the church age, when believers receive imperishable, glorious bodies suited for eternity. The "last trump" heralds this climactic moment, not the final trumpet of history, as trumpets will sound in the new heavens and earth (Revelation 8–11). This transformation fulfills the prophecy: "Death is swallowed up in victory. O death, where is thy sting? O grave, where is thy victory?" (1 Corinthians 15:54–55, KJV, citing Isaiah 25:8; Hosea 13:14). Christ's cross disarmed sin's sting, the power of death, and His resurrection guarantees our victory, ensuring that our glorified bodies will never again be subject to decay or sin.

## Conclusion: A Hope That Transforms

In a city skeptical of bodily resurrection, Paul reminded the Corinthians that the gospel—Christ's death, burial, and resurrection—is the foundation of their salvation and hope. This truth transforms a divided church into a unified body, living for eternity rather than fleeting status. A fireproof church stands firm in this gospel, abounding in God's work with the assurance of resurrection. As we conclude 1 Corinthians, may we embrace this hope, building a church that reflects Christ's victory over death.

## Application: Abounding in the Lord's Work

Paul concludes with a charge: "Therefore, my beloved brethren, be ye stedfast, unmoveable, always abounding in the work of the Lord, forasmuch as ye know that your labour is not in vain in the Lord" (1 Corinthians 15:58, KJV). The resurrection assures us that our efforts for Christ—despite trials, persecution, or physical pain—are not futile. Paul, bearing the scars of beatings and hardships (Galatians 6:17), exemplifies this, urging believers to pour their lives into God's work, confident in the eternal reward of a glorified body.

Here are four ways to apply this truth to build a fireproof church:

- **Stand Firm in the Gospel:** Hold fast to the truth of Christ's death, burial, and resurrection, letting it anchor your faith against cultural skepticism or doubt.

- **Share the Gospel Boldly:** Proclaim the gospel clearly, emphasizing Christ's atoning work and resurrection, inviting others to share in this hope.

185

- **Live with Resurrection Hope:** Let the promise of a glorified body inspire endurance through trials, knowing that present sufferings are temporary (Romans 8:18).

- **Abound in God's Work:** Serve the church tirelessly, as Paul did, trusting that your labor in Christ is never in vain, secured by the resurrection's certainty.

## Prayer

*Father, we thank You for the gospel—that Christ died for our sins, was buried, and rose again according to the Scriptures. Renew our hope in the resurrection, that we may abound in Your work, knowing our labor is not in vain. Draw those who have not believed to trust in Christ, sharing in this eternal hope. In Jesus' name,*

*Amen.*

# 16

## Finishing Well in Faith and Generosity

### From Heavenly Hope to Earthly Duty

In the soaring crescendo of 1 Corinthians 15, Paul unveiled the resurrection's triumph, declaring, "O death, where is thy sting? O grave, where is thy victory?" (1 Corinthians 15:55, KJV). This hope anchors the church in the promise of eternal life, transforming how believers live in a world that often mirrors Corinth's prideful, materialistic culture. As we explored in previous chapters, the Corinthian church grappled with division (Chapters 1–4), moral compromise (Chapters 5–6), chaotic worship (Chapters 11–14), and doubts about the resurrection (Chapter 15). Yet, Paul's letter does not end with doctrine alone. In 1 Corinthians 16, he turns to practical matters—generosity, service, steadfastness, and love—showing how a church rooted in the gospel translates heavenly hope into earthly duty.

Corinth, a city of commerce and competition, tempted believers to prioritize wealth and status over the self-sacrificial love of Christ (Keener, 1997, The IVP Bible

Background Commentary: New Testament, p. 492). In this final chapter of 1 Corinthians, Paul calls the church to finish well, living out the gospel through acts of generosity, support for faithful workers, and unwavering faith. For today's church, facing similar pressures of materialism and division, this chapter offers a blueprint for building a fireproof church—one that endures cultural fires by uniting in service and love. As we prepare for a concluding chapter that will call us to action, 1 Corinthians 16 equips us to live faithfully, reflecting the gospel's power in every aspect of church life.

## The Corinthian Context: A Call to Generosity in a Selfish City

Corinth's wealth, derived from its strategic position as a trade hub, fostered a culture of self-reliance and status-seeking, as noted in Chapter 1. Archaeological evidence, such as inscriptions honoring wealthy patrons, reveals a society where generosity was often a means to gain honor rather than serve others (Keener, 1997, p. 459). The Corinthian church, though transformed by the gospel, was not immune to these pressures. Some believers clung to their resources, mirroring the city's materialism, while others flaunted spiritual gifts to elevate themselves (1 Corinthians 14:26). Paul's instructions in 1 Corinthians 16 challenge this mindset, calling the church to a generosity that reflects Christ's self-giving love.

Paul begins with the collection for Jerusalem's poor believers: "Now concerning the collection for the saints, as I have given order to the churches of Galatia, even so do ye. Upon the first day of the week let every one of you lay by him in store, as God hath prospered him, that there be no gatherings when I come" (1 Corinthians 16:1–2, KJV). This collection, also mentioned in Romans 15:26 and 2 Corinthians 8–9, was a practical act of unity, linking the Gentile churches of Corinth and Galatia with the Jewish believers in Jerusalem, who faced poverty due to persecution and famine (Acts 11:28–30; Fee, 1987, The First Epistle to the Corinthians, NICNT, p. 813). By giving systematically—weekly, proportionate to their means—the Corinthians demonstrated that their faith extended beyond local concerns to the broader body of Christ.

This act of giving was not merely financial but an act of worship. Setting aside funds "upon the first day of the week" tied giving to the Lord's Day, when believers gathered to celebrate Christ's resurrection (Thiselton, 2000, The First Epistle to the Corinthians, NIGTC, p. 1321). In a city where wealth was a status symbol, Paul redirects the Corinthians to use their resources for God's glory, echoing the self-sacrificial love of Chapter 13: "Charity... seeketh not her own" (1 Corinthians 13:4–5, KJV). C.S. Lewis captures this principle in Mere Christianity: "The only safe rule is to give more than we can spare... If our charities do not at all pinch or hamper us, I should say they are too small" (Lewis, 1952, p. 86). For the Corinthians, and for us, generosity is a tangible expression of the gospel, uniting the church across cultures and needs.

## Faithful Service: Honoring God's Workers

Paul next commends those who serve the church faithfully: "I beseech you, brethren, (ye know the house of Stephanas, that it is the firstfruits of Achaia, and that they have addicted themselves to the ministry of the saints,) That ye submit yourselves unto such, and to every one that helpeth with us, and laboureth" (1 Corinthians 16:15–16, KJV). Stephanas, among the first converts in Achaia, led his household in selfless service, likely hosting the church and supporting its needs (1 Corinthians 1:16). The Greek term for "addicted" (*tasso*, to devote) suggests a deliberate, ongoing commitment to ministry, a stark contrast to Corinth's self-centered culture (Fee, 1987, p. 828). Paul urges the church to honor such workers, fostering mutual submission that strengthens unity.

Paul also addresses Timothy and Apollos: "Now if Timotheus come, see that he may be with you without fear: for he worketh the work of the Lord, as I also do. Let no man therefore despise him" (1 Corinthians 16:10–11, KJV).

Timothy, a young leader, faced potential rejection due to Corinth's earlier divisions over leaders like Apollos (1 Corinthians 1:12). Paul's defense of Timothy and his note that Apollos would visit later (16:12) show his care to heal factionalism, encouraging the church to welcome all who serve Christ. This call to honor faithful workers echoes Chapter 12's body metaphor, where every member contributes to the whole (1 Corinthians 12:12–27; Carson, 1994, New Bible Commentary, p. 1184).

For today's church, this challenges us to recognize and support those who labor in ministry—pastors, teachers, or unsung volunteers like Stephanas. In a culture that values fame, we must honor those who serve humbly, building a church where mutual respect overcomes division. As Lewis notes, "The work of a Beethoven, and the work of a charwoman, become spiritual on precisely the same condition, that of being offered to God" (Lewis, 1952, Mere Christianity, p. 87). Whether prominent or obscure, every act of service glorifies God when done for His sake.

## Steadfastness in Faith: Standing Firm in the Furnace

Paul's exhortations form the heart of the chapter: "Watch ye, stand fast in the faith, quit you like men, be strong. Let all your things be done with charity" (1 Corinthians 16:13–14, KJV). These five imperatives—

watch, stand fast, act courageously, be strong, and act in love—summarize the letter's call to resilience. "Watch" (*gregoreo*) implies vigilance against spiritual dangers, such as the false teachings or moral compromises addressed in Chapters 5–6 (Thiselton, 2000, p. 1333). "Stand fast in the faith" echoes Chapter 15's call to hold firm to the gospel (1 Corinthians 15:1–2), while "quit you like men" (*andrizomai*, act like men) urges courage, a military term fitting Corinth's competitive ethos. "Be strong" reinforces endurance, and "do all things in charity" ties every action to the love of Chapter 13.

These commands resonate with the book's theme of a fireproof church. Corinth's cultural pressures—materialism, pride, and division—mirror modern challenges like consumerism or theological drift. Paul's call to steadfastness empowers believers to resist these fires, grounded in the resurrection hope of Chapter 15: "Therefore, my beloved brethren, be ye stedfast, unmoveable, always abounding in the work of the Lord, forasmuch as ye know that your labour is not in vain in the Lord" (1 Corinthians 15:58, KJV). A fireproof church stands firm, not because of its own strength, but because Christ's victory over death guarantees the eternal value of its labor (Grudem, 2004, Evangelical Feminism and Biblical Truth, p. 297).

# Personal Connection: Paul's Pastoral Heart

Paul's personal plans and greetings reveal his pastoral care: "But I will tarry at Ephesus until Pentecost. For a great door and effectual is opened unto me, and there are many adversaries" (1 Corinthians 16:8–9, KJV). His decision to stay in Ephesus, despite opposition, models the steadfastness he urges, showing that ministry often requires perseverance through trials (Fee, 1987, p. 820). His greetings from Aquila and Priscilla and the Asian churches (16:19–20) foster a sense of global fellowship, reminding the Corinthians they are part of a larger body. The call to "greet one another with a holy kiss" (16:20, KJV) reflects cultural warmth, adapted today through handshakes or embraces, emphasizing community (Carson, 1994, p. 1185).

Paul's final warning is sobering: "If any man love not the Lord Jesus Christ, let him be Anathema Maranatha" (1 Corinthians 16:22, KJV). "Anathema" declares separation from those who reject Christ, while "Maranatha" ("Our Lord, come!") expresses longing for His return, tying to Chapter 15's resurrection hope (Thiselton, 2000, p. 1346). This dual note—judgment and hope—underscores Christ's centrality, ensuring the church's devotion remains fixed on Him.

# Living the Gospel: Lessons from Corinth

1 Corinthians 16 weaves together the threads of Paul's letter—unity, love, order, and hope—into a tapestry of practical faith. The collection teaches that generosity is worship, uniting believers across divides. Honoring workers like Stephanas and Timothy heals factionalism, reflecting Chapter 12's body. The call to steadfastness empowers the church to endure, rooted in Chapter 15's resurrection. Paul's pastoral care models the relational bonds that strengthen a fireproof church. As we face modern parallels to Corinth's materialism and division, these lessons equip us to live out the gospel faithfully.

Consider a small church in a bustling city, much like Corinth. Its members, tempted by career ambitions or cultural trends, might hoard resources or vie for prominence. Yet, inspired by 1 Corinthians 16, they commit to weekly giving for global missions, honor their volunteers, and stand firm against secular pressures. Their pastor, like Paul, encourages them through personal care, fostering a community where love prevails. This church becomes a beacon, proving that the gospel transforms even the most competitive hearts.

# Conclusion: A Church That Endures

1 Corinthians 16 is Paul's final charge to a church in the furnace of Corinth—a call to finish well through generosity, service, and steadfast faith. In a city driven by wealth and pride, Paul redirects the church to the gospel's priorities: giving to the needy, honoring the faithful, standing firm, and loving deeply. These actions forge a fireproof church, united and resilient, ready to shine as a witness to Christ. As we move to our concluding chapter, which will rally us to live out these truths, let 1 Corinthians 16 inspire us to abound in the work of the Lord, knowing our labor is not in vain.

# Application: Building a Fireproof Church

To build a fireproof church that finishes well, consider these applications:

- **Give Generously as Worship:** Set aside resources regularly, as the Corinthians did, to support the church and those in need. Let giving reflect Christ's sacrifice: "For ye know the grace of our Lord Jesus Christ, that, though he was rich, yet for your sakes he became poor" (2 Corinthians 8:9, KJV).

- **Honor Faithful Servants:** Recognize and support those who labor in ministry, from pastors to volunteers, fostering unity through mutual respect. As Chapter 12 teaches, every member's contribution matters (1 Corinthians 12:27).

- **Stand Firm in Faith:** Be vigilant against cultural pressures—materialism, division, or false teaching—holding fast to the gospel's truth, as Chapter 15 urges (1 Corinthians 15:1–2).

- **Live in Love:** Let every action—giving, serving, greeting—be done in charity, fulfilling Chapter 13's call to love that "never faileth" (1 Corinthians 13:8, KJV).

- **Long for Christ's Return:** Pray "Maranatha," living with the resurrection hope of Chapter 15, trusting that Christ's return will complete our redemption.

These applications prepare the church for the challenges of a Corinth-like world, setting the stage for a final call to action in this concluding chapter.

## Prayer

*Father, we thank You for Your Word, which transforms us from division to unity, from selfishness to generosity. Equip us to give sacrificially, honor Your servants, and stand firm in faith, all in love.*

*May we long for Christ's return, praying "Maranatha," as we build fireproof churches for Your glory. In Jesus' name,*

*Amen.*

# 17

## Conclusion: Building a Fireproof Church for Today's World

### The Corinthian Blueprint

In the furnace of Corinth—a city ablaze with pride, materialism, and division—Paul forged a church that could withstand the flames. Through 1 Corinthians, he addressed a congregation fractured by factions (Chapters 1–4), compromised by sin (Chapters 5–6), confused about relationships and liberty (Chapters 7–10), chaotic in worship (Chapters 11–14), and skeptical of the resurrection (Chapter 15). Yet, in Chapter 16, he showed how a church transformed by the gospel lives out its faith through generosity, service, and steadfastness. This journey, from division to unity, from doubt to hope, offers a blueprint for building a fireproof church—one that endures the cultural pressures of any age, including our own.

As we conclude our study of 1 Corinthians, we stand at a crossroads. The challenges facing today's church—polarization, consumerism, moral relativism, and skepticism—mirror Corinth's struggles. Yet, the gospel that united the Corinthians remains our anchor. This final chapter synthesizes the lessons of 1 Corinthians, weaving together its themes of unity, holiness, love, order, hope, and generosity into a vision for a church that shines as a beacon in a skeptical world. With practical steps and a call to action, we aim to equip believers to build fireproof churches, rooted in the truth of God's Word and ablaze with Christ's love.

## Synthesizing the Vision: A Fireproof Church

The heart of 1 Corinthians is the gospel: "For I delivered unto you first of all that which I also received, how that Christ died for our sins according to the scriptures; And that he was buried, and that he rose again the third day according to the scriptures" (1 Corinthians 15:3–4, KJV).

This gospel, introduced in Chapter 1, dismantles human pride with the wisdom of the cross: "For the preaching of the cross is to them that perish foolishness; but unto us which are saved it is the power of God" (1 Corinthians 1:18, KJV). In a Corinthian culture obsessed with status, Paul called the church to unity, rejecting factions over leaders like himself or Apollos (Chapters 1–4). This unity, as we saw, is not uniformity but a shared commitment to Christ, binding diverse members into one body (Chapter 12).

Holiness, addressed in Chapters 5–6, guards this unity. Paul urged the church to discipline sin and pursue purity, reflecting God's character in a city marked by immorality (Keener, 1997, The IVP Bible Background Commentary: New Testament, p. 465). Chapters 7–10 applied this to relationships and liberty, teaching believers to prioritize others' edification over personal freedom. Love, the "more excellent way" of Chapter 13, binds these together: "Charity never faileth" (1 Corinthians 13:8, KJV). This love, patient and selfless, fuels orderly worship (Chapter 14), ensuring gifts like prophecy edify the body (Fee, 1987, The First Epistle to the Corinthians, NICNT, p. 589).

The resurrection, the climax of Chapter 15, anchors this vision. Because Christ rose, "death is swallowed up in victory" (1 Corinthians 15:54, KJV), guaranteeing that our labor is not in vain (15:58). Chapter 16 translated this hope into action, calling for generosity, service, and steadfastness: "Watch ye, stand fast in the faith, quit you like men, be strong. Let all your things be done with charity" (1 Corinthians 16:13–14, KJV). Together, these themes form a fireproof church —one united in the gospel, holy in conduct, loving in action, orderly in worship, hopeful in resurrection, and generous in service (Carson, 1994, New Bible Commentary, p. 1160).

# Modern Challenges: Corinth's Mirror in Today's World

Corinth's struggles are strikingly familiar. Like their factions over leaders, our churches face polarization— divisions over politics, theology, or preferences threaten unity. Consumerism, akin to Corinth's materialism, tempts us to prioritize wealth over generosity, while moral relativism echoes their lax standards (Chapters 5–6).

Skepticism about truth, like doubts about the resurrection, challenges our faith in a post-Christian culture (Thiselton, 2000, The First Epistle to the Corinthians, NIGTC, p. 1176). Yet, 1 Corinthians offers timeless solutions, calling us to build churches that withstand these fires.

Consider a modern church in a bustling city, much like Corinth. Its members, divided over worship styles or social issues, argue rather than unite. Some hoard resources, mirroring Corinth's wealth-driven culture, while others doubt the relevance of biblical truth. Yet, inspired by 1 Corinthians, the pastor preaches the cross's wisdom, uniting the congregation around Christ. Small groups form to foster accountability, reflecting Chapter 12's body.

Members give sacrificially to support missions, echoing Chapter 16's collection. Through love and discipline, they become a fireproof church, shining as a witness to a divided world. This vision, grounded in 1 Corinthians, shows that the gospel can transform even the most fractured communities.

## Call to Action: Building the Fireproof Church

C.S. Lewis once wrote, "The Church exists for nothing else but to draw men into Christ, to make them little Christs. If they are not doing that, all the cathedrals, clergy, missions, sermons, even the Bible itself, are simply a waste of time" (Mere Christianity, 1952, p. 199). This captures the heart of 1 Corinthians: a church exists to reflect Christ, uniting believers in His love and truth. To build a fireproof church today, we must act on the lessons of Corinth, applying the gospel to every facet of church life. Here are five practical steps to make this vision a reality:

- **Unite Around the Gospel:** Let the cross be the center of your church's identity, as Paul urged: "For I determined not to know anything among you, save Jesus Christ, and him crucified" (1 Corinthians 2:2, KJV). Reject divisions over secondary issues—whether politics, music, or personalities—and rally around the gospel's truth. Form small groups where members study Scripture together, fostering unity through shared faith, as Chapter 12's body metaphor teaches.

202

- **Pursue Holiness with Grace:** Uphold biblical standards, as in Chapters 5–6, by addressing sin with discipline and love, not judgmentalism. Create a culture of accountability where members encourage one another to live holy lives, reflecting God's character. For example, mentor young believers to navigate cultural pressures, ensuring the church stands as a light in a morally confused world (Grudem, 2004, Evangelical Feminism and Biblical Truth, p. 297).

- **Live Out Love Practically:** Make love the heartbeat of your church, as Chapter 13 commands. Serve the community—feed the hungry, visit the lonely, support the struggling—showing that "charity suffereth long, and is kind" (1 Corinthians 13:4, KJV). Train leaders to model humility, prioritizing others' needs over personal agendas, as Paul did in Corinth (Fee, 1987, p. 835).

- **Worship Orderly and Edifyingly:** Follow Chapter 14's call to orderly worship, ensuring every sermon, song, and prayer builds up the body. Teach sound doctrine, as Paul did, grounding believers in Scripture to counter skepticism. Encourage all members to use their gifts—teaching, serving, giving—in ways that glorifyGod and strengthen the church (Carson, 1994, p. 1172).

- **Hope in the Resurrection:** Anchor your church in Chapter 15's resurrection hope, living with eternity in view. Preach Christ's victory over death, reminding believers that "your labour is not in vain in the Lord" (1 Corinthians 15:58, KJV). Inspire generosity, as in Chapter 16, by supporting missions and the needy, trusting that every act of faith has eternal impact (Thiselton, 2000, p. 1346).

These steps transform churches into fireproof communities—united, holy, loving, orderly, and hopeful. Imagine a church where members forgive past divisions, give sacrificially to global missions, and worship with reverence, all while longing for Christ's return. Such a church, like Corinth's, can shine in the darkest cultural furnaces.

## Conclusion: A Church That Shines

1 Corinthians is more than a letter to a first-century church; it is God's Word for us today, calling us to build fireproof churches that withstand the flames of division, materialism, and doubt. From the cross's wisdom to love's endurance, from holiness's call to resurrection's hope, Paul's words equip us to live as Christ's body in a broken world. As we act on these truths—uniting in the gospel, pursuing holiness, living in love, worshiping orderly, and hoping in Christ—we become churches that reflect His glory. Let us pray "Maranatha" (1 Corinthians 16:22, KJV), not only longing for Christ's

return but laboring now to build His kingdom, knowing that our work endures forever.

## Prayer

*Father, we thank You for the blueprint of 1 Corinthians, guiding us to build fireproof churches. Unite us in the gospel, sanctify us in holiness, fill us with love, order our worship, and anchor us in resurrection hope. Empower us to act—giving generously, serving humbly, standing firm—until Christ returns. May we pray "Maranatha" with lives that shine Your glory. In Jesus' name,*

*Amen.*

# Appendix 1: The "Cup of Blessing" in Biblical and Theological Context

The phrase "cup of blessing" appears explicitly in 1 Corinthians 10:16: "The cup of blessing which we bless, is it not the communion of the blood of Christ?" (KJV). It is central to understanding the Lord's Supper in 1 Corinthians 11:23–25, where Paul recounts Jesus' institution: "This cup is the new testament in my blood: this do ye, as oft as ye drink it, in remembrance of me" (1 Corinthians 11:25, KJV). In Chapter 11, we noted that Jesus retained the cup of blessing in the Lord's Supper to represent "His shed blood and the joy of our new relationship with God," a powerful insight that ties the cup to the themes of unity and hope.

The "cup of blessing" is not just a ritual element but a symbol of Christ's covenant, uniting believers as one body and pointing to the eschatological hope of His return.

Below, we will explore its meaning through four lenses: its Jewish Passover origins, its transformation in the Lord's Supper, its significance in the Corinthian context, and its role in building a fireproof church.

# Jewish Passover Origins

The "cup of blessing" originates in the Jewish Passover meal, which Jesus reinterpreted at the Last Supper to institute the Lord's Supper (1 Corinthians 11:23–25). In the 1st-century Passover Seder, four cups of wine were consumed, each tied to a promise of deliverance in Exodus 6:6–7 ("I will bring you out," "I will deliver you," "I will redeem you," "I will take you"). The third cup, known as the *kos shel berakhah* ("cup of blessing"), was drunk after the meal and accompanied by the *birkat hamazon*, a prayer of thanksgiving for God's provision (Joachim Jeremias, The Eucharistic Words of Jesus, 1966, 85–90; Gordon Fee, The First Epistle to the Corinthians, NICNT, 2014, 468–69). This prayer, rooted in Jewish tradition, might include words like: "Blessed are You, O Lord our God, King of the universe, who creates the fruit of the vine" (Mishnah, Berakhot 6:1). The cup symbolized God's covenant faithfulness, the joy of redemption from Egypt, and the communal bond of His people.

In the Passover, the cup of blessing was a high point, celebrating God's covenant relationship with Israel. As David Garland notes, "The cup was a communal act of gratitude, uniting the participants in the shared story of God's deliverance" (1 Corinthians, BECNT, 2003, 470). This communal aspect was critical: the Passover meal, shared in households, reinforced

Israel's identity as one people under God's covenant, a theme Jesus would amplify in the Lord's Supper.

## Transformation in the Lord's Supper

When Jesus instituted the Lord's Supper, He transformed the Passover, as we mentioned in Chapter 11: "He did not include the lamb, for our Lamb is slain already. He did not include the bitter herbs, because Christ took the bitterness for us. He kept... the cup of blessing to remind us of the life in His shed blood and the joy of our new relationship with God." At the Last Supper, Jesus took the cup of blessing—likely the third Passover cup—and declared, "This cup is the new testament in my blood" (1 Corinthians 11:25, KJV; cf. Luke 22:20). This act redefined the cup as a symbol of the new covenant, sealed by His sacrificial blood, fulfilling the Passover's promise of redemption (Hebrews 9:15; Jeremiah 31:31–34).

By retaining the cup of blessing, Jesus emphasized continuity with the Passover's theme of covenant while pointing to His ultimate sacrifice. As noted, the cup represents "His shed blood," which gives life (Leviticus 17:11; John 6:53–56) and "the joy of our new relationship with God," echoing the Passover's celebration of redemption but now centered on Christ's death and resurrection. Anthony Thiselton explains, "The cup of blessing in the Lord's Supper signifies participation in Christ's blood, uniting believers in the new covenant and its eschatological hope" (The First Epistle to the Corinthians, NIGTC, 2000, 768). The cup binds believers in *koinonia* (communion, 1 Corinthians 10:16), sharing in Christ's sacrifice and anticipating the wedding supper of the Lamb (Revelation 19:7–9). This dual focus— remembrance and hope—makes the cup a powerful symbol of unity and future glory.

## Significance in the Corinthian Context

In Corinth, the "cup of blessing" took on added weight due to the church's divisions and abuses at the Lord's Supper (1 Corinthians 11:17–34). As detailed in Chapter 11, Corinth's social hierarchy—wealthy elites with leisure versus slaves bound by long workdays— created disparities in church gatherings (Bradley, Slavery and Society at Rome, 1994, 57–60; Engels, Roman Corinth, 1990, 89–92).

Wealthier members, arriving early to house churches, consumed lavish meals during the Love Feast, leaving late-arriving slaves and poor members hungry (1 Corinthians 11:21–22). This desecrated the cup of blessing, meant to symbolize shared participation in Christ's blood and unity as one body (1 Corinthians 10:16–17).

209

The Love Feast, within which the Lord's Supper was celebrated, was a communal meal meant to embody *koinonia*, as described in Jude 12 ("feasts of charity," KJV) (Lampe, From Paul to Valentinus, 2003, 36–39). The cup of blessing, blessed with a prayer of thanksgiving, was the climax, uniting all in Christ's sacrifice. Yet, as Fee notes, "By turning the Lord's Supper into a private feast, the Corinthians violated the very *koinonia* the cup of blessing was meant to signify" (Fee, 589). Paul's rebuke—"What! Do you not have houses to eat and drink in? Or do ye despise the church of God, and shame them that have not?" (1 Corinthians 11:22, KJV)—highlights how their selfishness turned the cup of blessing into a symbol of division, not unity. His call to "tarry one for another" (11:33) and "discern the Lord's body" (11:29) restores the cup's purpose: a shared act of worship that unites all in Christ's blood and hope.

## The Cup of Blessing in a Fireproof Church

For a fireproof church, the cup of blessing is a powerful symbol of unity and hope, extinguishing the fires of division that plagued Corinth. The cup represents "the life in His shed blood and the joy of our new relationship with God." It reminds believers that Christ's blood has reconciled them to God and one another, creating a new covenant community (Ephesians 2:13–16). In the context of Chapter 11, the cup counters the selfishness of Corinth's wealthy, who shamed the poor, by calling all to share in Christ's sacrifice equally, regardless of status (Galatians 3:28). This unity strengthens the church's fireproof foundation in Christ (Chapter 4), ensuring it endures trials like social division or cultural pressure.

The cup also points to future hope, as Paul notes: "Ye do shew the Lord's death till he come" (1 Corinthians 11:26, KJV). This eschatological focus aligns with the Love Feast's anticipation of the wedding supper of the Lamb, where all believers—rich and poor, slave and free—will feast together in Christ's kingdom (Revelation 19:9). As Garland writes, "The cup of blessing is a foretaste of the eschatological banquet, uniting the church in hope and fellowship" (1 Corinthians, 471). A fireproof church drinks the cup with reverence, discerning the body (Christ's sacrifice and the church), and waits for one another, ensuring worship reflects the gospel's equality and joy.

# Appendix 2: The Role of Women in the Church: Reflecting God's Created Order

## A Vital Topic for a Unified Church

The role of women in the church is a vital issue for building a fireproof church that reflects God's design for unity and order, as explored throughout this book's exposition of 1 Corinthians. In Chapters 11 and 14, we addressed the Lord's Supper and orderly worship, touching on Paul's instructions regarding women in 1 Corinthians 11:1–16 and 14:26–40. These passages, often debated due to their cultural and theological complexity, require careful study to honor God's Word amidst Corinth's chaotic context and today's cultural pressures. This appendix offers a focused exploration of women's roles, affirming their active participation while upholding the divine order of headship established in creation. By grounding our understanding in Scripture and informed by evangelical scholarship, we aim to foster a church where all members—men and women—contribute to the body's edification under Christ's authority.

# The Corinthian Context: Order Amid Cultural Chaos

As detailed in Chapter 1, Corinth was a Roman colony steeped in competition and status-seeking, with a culture that valued public displays of prominence (Keener, 1997, The IVP Bible Background Commentary: New Testament, p. 459). This ethos infiltrated the church, leading to disorderly worship where believers, including women, competed for attention through spiritual gifts (1 Corinthians 14:26–33).

Greco-Roman norms often restricted women's public roles, yet some Corinthian women may have overstepped these boundaries, asserting authority in ways that disrupted worship (Fee, 1987, The First Epistle to the Corinthians, NICNT, p. 699). Paul's instructions in 1 Corinthians 11 and 14 address this chaos, not to silence women but to ensure worship reflects God's created order, promoting unity and edification (Carson, 1994, New Bible Commentary, p. 1172).

# Women's Participation in Worship

Paul affirms women's active role in worship: "But every woman that prayeth or prophesieth with her head uncovered dishonoureth her head: for that is even all one as if she were shaven" (1 Corinthians

11:5, KJV). Far from prohibiting speech, Paul assumes women will pray and prophesy publicly, provided they do so with a "covering" symbolizing submission to God's order (Grudem, 2004, Evangelical Feminism and Biblical Truth, p. 223). Prophecy, in the early church, often involved direct revelations, but with the New Testament's completion, it is now the proclamation of Scripture, a task open to all believers, including women, in appropriate settings (Fee, 1987, p. 589; see Chapter 14). Examples like Priscilla, who instructed Apollos alongside Aquila (Acts 18:26), and Philip's four daughters, who prophesied under their father's authority (Acts 21:9), demonstrate women's significant roles in sharing God's truth (Keener, 1997, p. 384).

These examples refute any notion that women were excluded from speaking. Rather, Paul's concern is the manner of their participation, ensuring it aligns with the divine order to avoid the chaos seen in Corinth's competitive worship (Thiselton, 2000, The First Epistle to the Corinthians, NIGTC, p. 830). Women today can teach and share Scripture in settings like women's groups or informal discussions, provided they respect the church's leadership structure, as Priscilla did under Aquila's partnership.

# The Principle of Headship

Paul grounds his teaching in creation: "But I would have you know, that the head of every man is Christ; and the head of the woman is the man; and the head of Christ is God" (1 Corinthians 11:3, KJV). The Greek term *kephale* (head) denotes both authority and source, reflecting the order in Genesis 2 (Grudem, 1985, JETS 28:3, pp. 275–294). In Genesis 2:7, God forms man from the dust, breathing life into him, and in Genesis 2:21–22, He creates woman from man's side: "And the man said, This is now bone of my bones, and flesh of my flesh: she shall be called Woman, because she was taken out of Man" (Genesis 2:23, KJV).

Woman is man's equal, a "help meet" (*ezer*, Genesis 2:18, KJV), designed as a partner to stand shoulder-to-shoulder, yet under man's leadership in specific contexts (Carson, 1994, p. 1168).

## This headship is not about superiority but responsibility.

In Genesis 3:6, Adam's failure to lead allows Eve to be deceived, disrupting God's order, with Adam compounding the error by blaming her (Genesis 3:12). Paul calls the church to reflect creation's order in worship, ensuring men and women work together to edify the body. The phrase "because of the angels"

(1 Corinthians 11:10, KJV) likely refers to angelic witnesses who observe worship, expecting it to reflect God's design (Ephesians 3:10; Keener, 1997, p. 473).

## Head Coverings: Principle vs. Custom

In Corinth, a head covering symbolized a woman's submission to her husband or father: "For if the woman be not covered, let her also be shorn: but if it be a shame for a woman to be shorn or shaven, let her be covered" (1 Corinthians 11:6, KJV). An uncovered head or shaved hair could signal immodesty or defiance in Corinthian culture, akin to rejecting her role (Fee, 1987, p. 512). Paul's concern is not the custom of veiling but the principle it represents: submission to God's created order. He notes mutual dependence: "Nevertheless neither is the man without the woman, neither the woman without the man, in the Lord. For as the woman is of the man, even so is the man also by the woman; but all things of God" (1 Corinthians 11:11–12, KJV), affirming equality in value (Thiselton, 2000, p. 841).

This distinction between principle and custom is key. Just as the "holy kiss" (1 Corinthians 16:20) or wine in communion reflects cultural practices we adapt today (e.g., handshakes, grape juice), head coverings are not mandatory, but the principle of submission remains. Women today honor this by respecting church leadership and God's design, not necessarily by wearing veils (Carson, 1994, p. 1170).

## Silence and Submission in Worship

Paul addresses disorderly worship in 1 Corinthians 14: "Let your women keep silence in the churches: for it is not permitted unto them to speak; but they are commanded to be under obedience, as also saith the law. And if they will learn any thing, let them ask their husbands at home: for it is a shame for a woman to speak in the church" (1 Corinthians 14:34–35, KJV). This "silence" does not mean total muteness, as 11:5 allows women to pray and prophesy. Rather, it likely addresses disruptive speech, such as interrupting to evaluate prophecies, which was a role reserved for male leaders in Corinth's context (Fee, 1987, p. 705). The call to ask husbands at home suggests private discussions to maintain order, fostering unity as couples address questions together (Thiselton, 2000, p. 1152).

Paul emphasizes that this principle applies "as in all churches of the saints" (1 Corinthians 14:33b, KJV), indicating a universal standard of order, not a Corinth-specific rule (Grudem, 2004, p. 245). Women are not to exercise authoritative teaching or correction over men in public worship, but they can contribute through prayer, prophecy, or teaching in settings like women's groups, as seen with Priscilla (Acts 18:26).

Submission is a voluntary choice (*hupotasso*, to submit willingly), not forced oppression, reflecting Christlike humility for the church's flourishing (Ephesians 5:21; Fee, 1987, p. 708).

## Application: Building a Fireproof Church

Paul's instructions challenge the church to reflect God's order while valuing women's contributions. Here are three ways to apply these truths:

- **Honor God's Created Order:** Men and women should embrace their roles, with men leading responsibly and women submitting voluntarily, reflecting the unity of Genesis 2:24.

- **Encourage Women's Participation:** Welcome women to pray, share Scripture, and teach in appropriate settings, as Priscilla did, ensuring their gifts edify the church under proper authority.

- **Pursue Orderly Worship:** Conduct services that prioritize edification and peace, as discussed in Chapter 14, with all members contributing in ways that honor God's design.

# Conclusion: A Church That Honors God's Design

In Corinth's competitive culture, Paul called the church to worship in a way that reflects God's created order, balancing women's active participation with the principle of submission. This fosters a unified, fireproof church where all members work together to glorify Christ. By grounding our practices in Scripture, we build a church that stands firm against cultural pressures, honoring God's Word as Paul commanded: "If any man think himself to be a prophet, or spiritual, let him acknowledge that the things that I write unto you are the commandments of the Lord" (1 Corinthians 14:37, KJV).

[1] The phrase "as also saith the law" (1 Corinthians 14:34, KJV) is ambiguous, as no Old Testament verse explicitly commands women's silence in worship. It likely refers to creation principles (Genesis 2:18–24) or Jewish cultural norms of submission, as interpreted by some scholars (Keener, 1997, p. 487).

Bibliography

Carson, D.A. *New Bible Commentary*. IVP Academic, 1994.

Fee, Gordon D. *The First Epistle to the Corinthians. New International Commentary on the New Testament* (NICNT), Eerdmans, 1987.

Grudem, Wayne. *Evangelical Feminism and Biblical Truth*. Crossway, 2004.

Grudem, Wayne. *"The Meaning of Kephalē ('Head'): A Response to Recent Studies."* Journal of the Evangelical Theological Society (JETS), vol. 28, no. 3, 1985, pp. 275–294.

Keener, Craig S. *The IVP Bible Background Commentary: New Testament*. InterVarsity Press, 1997.

Thiselton, Anthony C. *The First Epistle to the Corinthians. New International Greek Testament Commentary* (NIGTC), Eerdmans, 2000.

Jeremias, Joachim. *The Eucharistic Words of Jesus*. SCM Press, 1966.

Garland, David E. *1 Corinthians. Baker Exegetical Commentary on the New Testament* (BECNT), Baker Academic, 2003.

Lampe, Peter. *From Paul to Valentinus: Christians at Rome in the First Two Centuries.* Fortress Press, 2003.

Bradley, Keith R. *Slavery and Society at Rome.* Cambridge University Press, 1994.

Engels, Donald W. *Roman Corinth: An Alternative Model for the Classical City.* University of Chicago Press, 1990.

Frier, Bruce W. *A Natural History of Roman Life.* Oxford University Press, 2000.

Lewis, C.S. *Mere Christianity.* HarperOne, 1952.

# About the Author

James Burke is the senior pastor of Grace Community Church in Marinette, Wisconsin. With a passion for preaching God's Word and shepherding God's people, he has spent decades helping believers grow in faith and guiding churches toward gospel-centered health. His ministry is marked by a commitment to Scripture, a love for Christ's church, and a desire to see lives transformed by the power of the cross. When he isn't preaching or writing, James enjoys time with his wife Roxanne, meaningful conversations over coffee, and the beauty of life along the shores of Lake Michigan.

www.ingramcontent.com/pod-product-compliance
Lightning Source LLC
Chambersburg PA
CBHW070913130626
46555CB00001B/117